PEOPLE
IN THE NEWS

George Lucas

by Adam Woog

Lucent Books, San Diego, CA

Titles in the People in the News series include:

Garth Brooks	Rosie O'Donnell
Jim Carrey	Colin Powell
Bill Gates	Christopher Reeve
John Grisham	The Rolling Stones
Jesse Jackson	Steven Spielberg
Michael Jordan	R. L. Stine
Stephen King	Oprah Winfrey
George Lucas	Tiger Woods
Dominique Moceanu	

For my wife Karen, even though I couldn't convince her that watching all of George Lucas's movies was strictly for research.

Library of Congress Cataloging-in-Publication Data

Woog, Adam, 1953–
    George Lucas / Adam Woog.
        p. cm. — (People in the news)
    Includes bibliographical references and index.
    Summary: Examines the personal life, career, and success of the creator of the "Star Wars" and "Indiana Jones" movies, whose technological innovations have had a major impact on the film industry.
    ISBN 1-56006-434-X (lib. bdg. : alk. paper)
    1. Lucas, George—Juvenile literature. 2. Motion picture producers and directors—United States Biography Juvenile literature.
    [1. Lucas, George. 2. Motion picture producers and directors.]
    I. Title. II. Series: People in the news (San Diego, Calif.)
PN1998.3.L835W66   2000
791.43'028'092—dc21
[B]   99-31964
                                                                          CIP

Table of Contents

Foreword

FAME AND CELEBRITY are alluring. People are drawn to those who walk in fame's spotlight, whether they are known for great accomplishments or for notorious deeds. The lives of the famous pique public interest and attract attention, perhaps because their experiences seem in some ways so different from, yet in other ways so similar to, our own.

Newspapers, magazines, and television regularly capitalize on this fascination with celebrity by running profiles of famous people. For example, television programs such as *Entertainment Tonight* devote all of their programming to stories about entertainment and entertainers. Magazines such as *People* fill their pages with stories of the private lives of famous people. Even newspapers, newsmagazines, and television news frequently delve into the lives of well-known personalities. Despite the number of articles and programs, few provide more than a superficial glimpse at their subjects.

Lucent's People in the News series offers young readers a deeper look into the lives of today's newsmakers, the influences that have shaped them, and the impact they have had in their fields of endeavor and on other people's lives. The subjects of the series hail from many disciplines and walks of life. They include authors, musicians, athletes, political leaders, entertainers, entrepreneurs, and others who have made a mark on modern life and who, in many cases, will continue to do so for years to come.

These biographies are more than factual chronicles. Each book emphasizes the contributions, accomplishments, or deeds that have brought fame or notoriety to the individual and shows how that person has influenced modern life. Authors portray their subjects in a realistic, unsentimental light. For example, Bill Gates—the cofounder and chief executive officer of the software giant Microsoft—has been instrumental in making personal computers the most vital tool of the modern age. Few dispute his business savvy, his perseverance, or his technical expertise, yet critics say he is ruthless in his dealings with competitors and driven more by his desire to maintain Microsoft's dominance in the computer industry than by an interest in furthering technology.

In these books, young readers will encounter inspiring stories about real people who achieved success despite enormous obstacles. Oprah Winfrey—the most powerful, most watched, and wealthiest woman on television today—spent the first six years of her life in the care of her grandparents while her unwed mother sought work and a better life elsewhere. Her adolescence was colored by promiscuity, pregnancy at age fourteen, rape, and sexual abuse.

Each author documents and supports his or her work with an array of primary and secondary source quotations taken from diaries, letters, speeches, and interviews. All quotes are footnoted to show readers exactly how and where biographers derive their information and provide guidance for further research. The quotations enliven the text by giving readers eyewitness views of the life and accomplishments of each person covered in the People in the News series.

In addition, each book in the series includes photographs, annotated bibliographies, timelines, and comprehensive indexes. For both the casual reader and the student researcher, the People in the News series offers insight into the lives of today's newsmakers—people who shape the way we live, work, and play in the modern age.

Introduction

Building Dreams and Empires

Making movies is like being able to cement dreams in concrete and then dig them up again a hundred years later and say, "Oh, this is what they were dreaming about in those days."
—George Lucas

*S*TAR *WARS* WAS a project that seemed to have little chance of being noticed. It was a science fiction fantasy, a genre Hollywood had not had much success with. Its production had been low-budget, chaotic, and uncertain. It opened in only a few theaters and with virtually no advance publicity. No one, not even its creator, George Lucas, thought the movie would amount to much.

Instead, the film became part of the fabric of popular culture immediately upon its release in 1977. The movie combined a moral message and heartfelt emotion with amazing special effects and swashbuckling action. Lucas brought together a mix of sources, ranging from fairy tales and myths to TV westerns and adventure comic books, to create a timeless creative statement.

Star Wars was, for years, the biggest movie in history, and it has remained one of the most enduring movies of all time. But it was more than just another surprise box office hit; the film became a genuine phenomenon. Its characters and dialogue entered the worldwide cultural mainstream; people everywhere began speaking of "the Force" and "the dark side."

Its astonishing success actually changed the way movies are produced. Furthermore, the success of *Star Wars* made the movie's director, until then just one of several promising young directors trying to catch a break, into a celebrity and a legend.

Blockbusters

Lucas has created only a handful of films besides *Star Wars.* Furthermore, for decades the stubbornly independent film-maker has distanced himself as much as possible from the Hollywood mainstream. Nonetheless, he has perhaps done more than any other single person to change the nature of the film industry.

Star Wars changed how Hollywood studios want movies to perform at the box office. Today, the vast majority of commercial films are designed to become huge blockbusters. Blockbusters—often called popcorn movies to differentiate them from more serious cinematic fare—typically mimic the recipe perfected by Lucas: heavy on swift action and splashy special effects, aiming to draw in specific age groups, opening (as did the sequels to *Star Wars*) at thousands of theaters simultaneously, and backed by enormous promotional campaigns.

C3PO and R2-D2, two of George Lucas's android characters, on the set of Star Wars.

"Any Ideas?"

In his introduction to Charles Champlin's book *George Lucas: The Creative Impulse*, Steven Spielberg comments on Lucas and his films.

> Lucasfilm touches our lives from many different directions, descending upon our eyes, our ears, and our children. George has never stopped asking, "Any ideas?" and the whole world has been a better place for it. For two decades I've tried to figure out George's genius. I have tried to unearth it as though it were some archaeological antiquity—George Lucas's crystal ball. After much thought, the only explanation I can offer is this: one day, in a brilliant flash of white light, he saw the future, and he has spent the last twenty years showing it to us.

Lucas's friend and sometime collaborator Steven Spielberg says that *Star Wars* shook the establishment up in a positive way. According to Spielberg, the movie forced Hollywood to expand its worldview, so that its films now embrace universal human values that can be understood and appreciated by everyone. He remarks, "*Star Wars* was a seminal moment when the entire industry instantly changed. For me, it's when the world recognized the value of childhood."[1]

However, many observers are critical of the blockbuster trend. They argue that blockbusters represent Hollywood's worst excesses, filmmaking at its dreariest and most mindless. Also, because blockbusters are so expensive to produce, they will not be profitable unless they bring in enormous returns. This means that entire studios can succeed or fail on the strength of a single film.

Furthermore, critics charge, the trend means that smaller films are ignored, or not even made, in the rush to produce monster hits. Speaking of *Star Wars* and Spielberg's *Jaws*, critic David Thomson complains, "These films did such business that the business itself shifted its focus. As never before, it [Hollywood] developed disdain for 'small' pictures."[2]

Lucas does not accept responsibility for the blockbuster mentality. He points out that no one is forcing audiences to see his movies, so he must be doing something right. He is proud of his reputation as a careful, financially conservative filmmaker who always brings in his projects on budget. The bloated excess of recent "popcorn" movies, he says, is due to the extravagances of studio executives who waste vast sums on poor material: "They've been trying to do blockbusters since *Gone with the Wind.* Bad movies have been around since the beginning of time. The notion that I'm responsible for them is totally unfair."[3]

The Rise of Special Effects

But if Lucas did not launch the blockbuster movement, he did help change the film world in other ways. His innovative use of sophisticated special effects pioneered a renaissance of a genre, science fiction/fantasy, which, with a few exceptions, had fallen into disrepute in Hollywood. The history of special effects technology, in fact, can be neatly divided into the periods before and after *Star Wars.*

Before *Star Wars,* special effects were a relatively crude and obscure subarea of filmmaking. One or two trick shots, if any, might be required in a film. After *Star Wars,* however, special effects began to dominate Hollywood; and dozens of films, good and bad, relied heavily on ever more sophisticated visual images. The Academy of

Motion Picture Arts and Sciences even set up a new Oscar award to honor the creators of the best special effects each year.

At their best, special effects can help creative minds put on screen the spectacular visions they can otherwise only dream about. Lucas himself has

George Lucas, who began his career by directing low-budget films, has become one of the most influential directors of our time.

gone back to improve what he felt were incomplete or crudely made shots in his earlier movies. He has also spent much of the last two decades pioneering refinements in cutting-edge effects technology.

Lucas acknowledges that technology is not the complete answer, pointing out that no movie can rely on effects alone, but must be balanced by character development and depth of plot. Nonetheless, the latest uses of technology in filmmaking, Lucas feels, will have an enormous impact on cinema history. "Digital technology is the same revolution as adding sound to pictures and the same revolution as adding color to pictures," he says. "Nothing more, nothing less."[4]

Besides *Star Wars*

Lucas has never really liked directing movies. The 1999 release of *Star Wars Episode One: The Phantom Menace*, the first installment of a planned trilogy of new *Star Wars* films, marked the first time he has sat in the director's chair since *Star Wars*.

However, Lucas has not been idle during the two decades between those films. During that time he produced two sequels to *Star Wars*, as well as three movies with his friend Spielberg about the consummate swashbuckler Indiana Jones. All were wildly successful in both financial and artistic terms. Lucas produced a number of other films that had mixed financial and critical success, and was active in other areas of filmmaking.

An Interesting Combination

Carroll Ballard, the director of *The Black Stallion*, knows George Lucas well. In Dale Pollock's *Skywalking: The Life and Films of George Lucas*, he has this to say about his friend's ability to mix a wide-eyed sense of wonder with a mature business sense.

When you meet George, he seems interested in very simple things. He's still living in his childhood in a certain way. He's able to reach back there and remember it vividly and share it. He can make sense of those things and sell them. But he's also a man of the world, a guy who really knows about money, is very calculating and business-oriented. He's a very interesting combination of both.

George Lucas (right) and Steven Spielberg (left) place their hands in cement in front of Mann's Chinese Theater, May 6, 1984.

The filmmaker also survived a painful divorce to become the devoted single father of three, raising his children in the relative seclusion of their northern California home. Throughout it all, meanwhile, he guided the creation of a remarkable empire of his own.

Lucas was one of the first filmmakers to fully grasp the merchandising possibilities for toys, books, and other products related to a movie. Accordingly, he always retains the rights to produce and market these products. As the vast universe of *Star Wars* merchandising steadily expanded, the profits made Lucas and his primary company, Lucasfilms, extremely wealthy.

Lucas has spent relatively little of that wealth on himself, however. He lives well, but not extravagantly. Instead, he has chosen to reinvest his profits in companies that are on the technological cutting edge of the film industry. The most visible result of this is nestled in an idyllic country setting in northern California: Skywalker Ranch is a state-of-the-art film studio still

"You Can Make a Difference"

In "Luke Skywalker Goes Home," an interview by Bernard Weinraub published in *Playboy* magazine in 1997, Lucas reflects on the themes that run through his movies.

My films have a tendency to promote a personal self-esteem, a you-can-do-it attitude. Their message is, "Don't listen to everyone else. Discover your own feelings and follow them. Then you can overcome anything." It's old-fashioned and very American. . . . All [people who are drifting] need is the inspiration to say, "Don't let all this get you down. You can do it.". . . It's the one thing I discovered early on. You may have to overcome a lot of fear and get up a lot of courage, sometimes to do even the simplest things, sometimes to just get up in the morning. But you can do it. You can make a difference. Dreams are extremely important. You can't do it unless you imagine it.

in the making. The ranch is the fulfillment of Lucas's longtime dream: to make movies away from what he calls Hollywood's "sleaze factor."

Not bad, all things considered, for someone who grew up as the son of a stationery store owner in the small town of Modesto, California—and was barely aware of movies until he got to college.

Chapter 1

Modesto: A Long Time Ago in a Galaxy Far, Far Away . . .

I'm so ordinary that a lot of people can relate to me, because it's the same kind of ordinary that they are. I think it gives me an insight into the mass audience. I know what I liked as a kid, and I still like it.

—George Lucas

If there is a bright center to the universe, then this is the planet farthest from it.

—Luke Skywalker in *Star Wars*

MODESTO, CALIFORNIA, EAST of San Francisco and south of Sacramento, was a bustling, booming place during the Gold Rush of the 1800s. By the twentieth century, however, it had settled down to being just another typical small town of the region: hot, flat, and dusty. The area's main crops were walnuts and wine grapes, and Modesto itself was quiet and unassuming. People joked that it lived up to its name.

A Family Rooted in the Great Depression

George Lucas's father, George Walton Lucas Senior, arrived in this out-of-the-way spot in 1929 by the age of sixteen. He was already the sole breadwinner and the only male in his family. His father, an oil field worker, had died the year before.

13

While still in high school, George met Dorothy Bomberger, the privileged daughter of one of Modesto's most prominent and wealthy families. Despite the differences in their backgrounds, the two were attracted to each other and were married less than four years later.

America was in the depths of the Great Depression, a devastating economic slump that had begun in 1929. Jobs were scarce, but George found work at a stationery store owned by L. M. Morris, from whom he eventually bought the business. George expanded the store's stock to include office equipment, typewriters, and toys. He worked long hours, six days a week, and the store prospered.

George had conservative values and did not allow his wife to work, although she did help at home with the shop's bookkeeping. Instead, Dorothy concentrated on raising her two daughters: Ann, born in 1934, and Katherine, born in 1936.

Unfortunately, Dorothy's health began to decline. Although the problem was never completely identified, doctors suspected a disease of the pancreas. Her poor health required long periods of hospitalization and recovery at home, and her doctors advised her to have no more children. When she became pregnant again, it surprised everyone.

"Georgie" Is Born

George Walton Lucas Junior was born on May 14, 1944. The child inherited his father's black hair, pointed chin, dark eyes, and prominent ears. He also had his father's slim frame; Georgie, as he was nicknamed, was a small infant, and by age six still weighed only thirty-five pounds.

A housekeeper, Mildred Shelley, nicknamed Till, was hired when Georgie was eight months old, mainly because of his mother's poor health. Till, a gregarious southerner, became a second mother to Georgie and to Wendy, another "surprise" child born three years after Georgie.

Georgie, the family's only boy, was in many ways pampered as he grew up. George Senior was a strict disciplinarian, but he often complained that the Lucas women spoiled his son.

As a youth, Lucas spent many hours drawing landscapes and building extensive miniature cities.

In many ways, the boy's early childhood was idyllic. Nonetheless, he sometimes experienced anxieties and problems. He was often picked on by bigger kids, who devised such tortures as throwing his shoes into walnut grove sprinklers on the way home from school. He recalls,

> I was very much aware that growing up wasn't pleasant, it was just . . . frightening.

> I remember that I was unhappy a lot of the time. Not really unhappy—I enjoyed my childhood. But I guess all kids, from their point of view, feel depressed and intimidated. Although I had a great time, my strongest impression was that I was always on the lookout for the evil monster that lurked around the corner.[5]

Solitary

George was a quiet boy and rarely showed his emotions or thoughts to others. Even his sister Wendy, who spent a great deal of time with him when they were young, has admitted recently that she feels she never knew him well.

By nature a self-reliant child, intensely visual, and always something of a loner, George often withdrew into solitary pursuits. He spent hours drawing landscapes or creating elaborate miniature farms and cities, complete with tiny, meticulously crafted trucks and buildings. He also loved taking machines apart and putting them back together. His family remembers George as unusually persistent with all these projects, doggedly finishing whatever he started.

Despite these solitary pursuits, George also spent time with others. He and his sister Wendy were close, and he played for long hours with two good friends, John Plummer and George Frankenstein. Their pastimes included riding bicycles, building backyard carnivals, and playing with the latest toys from George Senior's store.

Another favorite pastime was reading comic books. John Plummer's father knew the owner of Modesto's newsstand, and the kids were allowed to collect unsold comics for free. George and Wendy had their own playhouse behind the Lucas house, with one room entirely devoted to their comic collection.

All in all, Lucas recalls, it was an ideal childhood, free from many of the stresses of city life. He says, "Even though it's California, it was a quiet Midwestern kind of upbringing. There wasn't much going on."[6]

TV Arrives

John Plummer's family was one of the first in Modesto to get a TV set, and George became an immediate convert. In the early 1950s, he visited the Plummers' house as often as possible, avidly watching cartoons and adventure shows in fuzzy black and white on the single channel available in Modesto.

When the Lucas family purchased their own set, in 1954, it was mounted on a revolving stand. George could watch in the living room after school, turn it around to watch during dinner, then turn it back to watch in the living room afterward. He loved old movies and westerns like *Gunsmoke*, but his favorite show was *Adventure Theater*. Every night from 6 to 6:30, George would drape his pet cat Dinky over his shoulders and settle in.

Adventure Theater mostly showed movie serials from the 1930s and 1940s. These short films had originally been shown in theaters, one episode at a time, before the main feature. Starring heroes with names like Spy Smasher, Tailspin Tommy, and the Masked Marvel, they were cliff-hangers—so called because each episode ended at a desperate point for the hero and left the audience eager to see the next installment.

The best of them all, in George's opinion, was *Flash Gordon Conquers the Universe*. In this classic, the fearless spaceman Flash Gordon, along with his sweetheart Dale Arden and their colleague Dr. Zharkov, battled the evil space tyrant Ming the Merciless.

George loved *Flash Gordon*'s flamboyant costumes, flaming rockets, and corny dialogue. It and other serials, he later commented, became a primary influence on his creative work as an adult. "The way I see things, the way I interpret things, is influenced by television. Visual conception, fast pace, quick cuts. I can't help it. I'm a product of the television age."[7]

A scene from Adventure Theater's Flash Gordon Conquers the Universe *which greatly influenced Lucas's work.*

"Bored Silly"

A high point of George's childhood was a visit to Disneyland. He was eleven when the famous theme park opened in 1956, and George and his pals were among the first to pass through its gates. After that, the Lucas family made an annual, week-long visit to Disneyland. George couldn't get enough of its imaginative use of fantasy and visual effects, an influence that, like TV and comics, would become important later.

There were other pastimes. George joined the Cub Scouts, played Little League baseball, and always rode his bike in Modesto's annual Fourth of July parade. In general, though, George was never athletic (and still is not); his father later recalled that as a child he was "a scrawny little devil."[8]

The Lucases made young George take music and dance lessons. He hated both, and he disliked attending services at the Methodist church on Sundays with the rest of the family. However, he loved to listen to music, whether on the radio or the record player.

Lucas was among Disneyland's first visitors when the theme park opened in 1956.

Committed

In this passage from Michael Pye and Lynda Myles's book *The Movie Brats*, Lucas reflects on the sense of commitment he acquired as a boy in Modesto:

> I never have thought of myself as being very smart. Once I commit myself to something, however, I'm really committed. I'll carry it through to the end. . . . The secret to my success is the fact that I work harder than anybody else.

At John Muir Elementary School, George took part in school plays, sang in the choir, and served on safety patrol. He was an indifferent student, notoriously poor at spelling, and his grades were rarely better than C's. According to family legend, Wendy rose early every morning to correct her brother's spelling lessons before school. Lucas's spelling and grammar are still poor. "I'm not the greatest speller," he admits. "I'm horrible at math. I just never considered myself intelligent in the academic sense." [9]

Throughout his years at Roosevelt Junior High and Thomas Downey High School, George did well in art, but consistently received mediocre grades in science and English. He even failed arithmetic and spelling in eighth grade and had to repeat them during the summer. He admits freely that he was unengaged by academics, saying simply, "I was bored silly." [10]

Buzz Versus His Dad

When George was fifteen, the Lucases moved to a big farm-house on thirteen acres of walnut trees. George hated leaving the old neighborhood and threatened to run away, but eventually grew to love the new place. It had plenty of room in which he could roam and find solitude. Sometimes this meant avoiding his father.

Life in the Lucas household was always strict. Because Dorothy's illnesses prevented her from playing an active role in the family, her husband dominated the children's lives. George Senior sometimes displayed an unexpected sense of humor, but generally his iron will and somber bearing proved intimidating.

George's friend John Plummer recalls, "Every time Mr. Lucas came around, you just kind of hid."[11]

George Senior's role in his son's life often seemed overwhelming. He had high expectations for his only son, and often imposed his will against his son's wishes. In one especially humiliating summer ritual, George Senior shaved off his son's hair, a practice that gave rise to the hated nickname Buzz.

As George grew older, the tensions between father and son increased. They had little in common, and George seemed disinclined to enter the stationery business. Furthermore, George seemed unable to impress his tough-minded father, and George Senior seemed unable to express pride in his son. "George never listened to me," George Senior complained, years after his boy had become a world-famous celebrity and one of the wealthiest people alive. "He was his mother's pet."[12]

Three Passions

Three passions consumed George during his high school years. One was music: classic rock and roll, the defining pop music of the time, captivated him. He spent hours in his room listening to singers like Elvis Presley and Chuck Berry while doing his

Elvis Presley, whose music and style appealed to Lucas.

Outwitted

Despite his own intentions, Lucas is still, in many ways, guided by the values he learned from his father, as the filmmaker comments in this excerpt from a 1997 profile by John Seabrook in *The New Yorker*, "Why Is the Force Still with Us?"

My father provided me with a lot of business principles—a small-town retail-business ethic, and I guess I learned it. It's sort of ironic, because I swore when I was a kid I'd never do what he did. At eighteen, we had this big break, when he wanted me to go into the business and I refused, and I told him, "There are two things I know for sure. One is that I will end up doing something with cars, whether I'm a racer, a mechanic, or whatever, and, two, that I will never be president of a company." I guess I got outwitted.

homework, reading comic books, and consuming Hershey bars and Cokes. George started dressing like his idols, too, slicking his hair back with gobs of Vaseline, refusing to wash his jeans, and wearing sharp-pointed black shoes.

Another passion was photography, an interest that began when his parents gave him a 35-millimeter still camera and deepened after his father helped him convert a spare bathroom into a darkroom. George took all kinds of pictures, but he especially liked to shoot race cars and crop-dusting planes in action. Sometimes the planes flew so low that he could photograph the pilots as they swooped by.

George's greatest passion, however, was reserved for fast cars. He got his first auto at fifteen, before he could legally drive. It was a used Italian-built Fiat Balanchina, a tiny machine with a two-cylinder engine. George Senior thought his son would be safe in a little car without much power, but George modified it to make it faster. George failed the test for his license the first time because he was careless about the rules. Even after passing, he ignored speed limits regularly and racked up many tickets.

"Wheels," Lucas recalls, gave new hope to his otherwise dull high school life: "I had my own life once I had my car. Along with the sense of power and freedom came the competitiveness to see who was the fastest, who was the craziest, and who was the bravest." [13]

Cruising

George began entering, and often winning, local races. Racing was a sport in which he could excel despite his size. In fact, his light weight and small frame were definite advantages in the little cockpit of his car, and George soon began to entertain the notion of becoming a professional driver.

He also considered using his drawing skills to become an artist specializing in race cars. At the very least, he thought, he would become a mechanic—anything, as long as it had to do with cars. His below-average grades, he knew, were not going to get him a great job. All through high school, George remained immersed in cars and California's car culture. A major part of this was the ritual pastime called cruising.

Modesto was a major cruising town, drawing kids from other small towns all around. Almost every night for four years, and all day on the weekends, George and his buddies drove slowly up and down Modesto's main streets, admiring each other's cars, stopping for burgers, and trying to pick up girls. "Nobody knew who I was," Lucas recalls about his dating efforts. "I'd say, 'Hi, I'm George,' but after that night I'd never see the girls again."[14]

Gangs were a looming presence in this scene, all of which he would recreate later on film. Although never a member of any gang, George was friendly with a group called the Faros. The threat of getting beat up was constant for a little guy like George, and knowing the Faros was good insurance. Lucas recalls, "The

A Workaholic Who Works Alone

In this passage from Dale Pollock's *Skywalking*, George Lucas Senior (who has since passed away) reflects on some of the qualities that form his own personality, which he seems to have passed on to his filmmaker son:

I'm kind of a perfectionist, I guess. To some extent I neglected my family. For years, I was at work at seven A.M., six days a week. I wouldn't quit until I had done something to my satisfaction, and I never wanted to lose. I was a loner—I didn't want to take anyone else on, because if I got into trouble I'd bring them down with me.

only way to keep from getting [beat up] was to hang out with some really tough guys who happened to be your friends." [15]

The Crash

On the day George was to have graduated from high school in 1962, a terrifying car accident nearly killed him and put an end to his dreams of becoming a professional driver.

While turning the little Fiat into his driveway, George was struck broadside by a speeding car. The other driver was barely hurt, but George's car rolled over four or five times before slamming into a walnut tree so hard that the tree was uprooted and carried several feet. George's special racing seat belt snapped, a malfunction that saved his life. Because it broke, he was thrown clear of the wreck; if he had been in the car when it hit the tree, he would surely have died.

George's injuries included serious puncture damage to his lungs as well as damage to one shoulder and several ribs. He made a full recovery, although he received his high school diploma in the hospital. He spent the rest of the summer at home recuperating, with daily trips to the hospital for physical therapy.

The crash proved to be a major turning point in Lucas's life. Until then, he had more or less drifted along, never applying himself to a task unless it interested him and disregarding his father's stern warnings that he would never amount to anything. The accident shook him out of this aimlessness, forcing him to realize the fragile and fleeting nature of life. He recalls:

> I realized that [by racing] I'd been living my life so close to the edge for so long. That's when I decided to go straight, to be a better student, to try to do something with myself. You can't have that kind of experience and not feel that there must be a reason why you're here. I realized I should be spending my time trying to figure out what that reason is and trying to fulfill it. [16]

George's search for meaning led him to an environment that would allow him to blossom: film school.

Chapter 2

Film School

With a camera and an editing machine, you can move people to tears.

—George Lucas

This was a guy who never had any direction before, and now suddenly he had asserted himself and became totally devoted to one thing, film.
—George Lucas's childhood friend John Plummer

Lucas's grades were not good enough to gain him admission to a four-year college, but he was accepted at Modesto Junior College. Fired up about studying for the first time in his life, he developed special interests in sociology, anthropology, English literature, and creative writing.

College was hard work, but Lucas persevered and the effort was reflected in his grades: an A in astronomy, B's in speech, sociology, and art history. In the spring of 1964, he received his AA (associate in arts) degree.

Film School Beckons

While in junior college, George received a present from his father: an 8-millimeter movie camera, and Lucas became as intrigued with film as he had with still photography. In particular, he began filming race cars; his accident had cured him of becoming a pro driver, but it had not taken away his enthusiasm for fast cars.

Making movies, at this point, was still just a hobby. Lucas's entry into the world of serious filmmaking came almost by accident.

Interested in more college, he investigated several schools. His childhood friend John Plummer, who was attending the University of Southern California in Los Angeles, suggested that USC's cinema department, the oldest and largest film school in the country, might be interesting.

Encouragement and aid came from Haskell Wexler, a Hollywood cameraman and auto-racing fan known to George through racing connections. Wexler, who would play an important role in Lucas's life in later years, phoned some friends at USC's film school and urged them to help Lucas's entrance application along.

Lucas has said in later years that he did not have any clear ideas about what he was going to do when he applied to film school; he was, he says, simply following his instincts. He had vague ideas about doing something creative, and at the very least he was eager to get away from Modesto and the constricting influence of his father.

"A Great Example for Parents"

George Senior was deeply unhappy when his son was accepted by USCinema, as the university's film department was called. The elder Lucas liked the idea that his son had been accepted by a prestigious school, but he was mistrustful of what he perceived USC to be: a cesspool of hustlers and useless intellectuals.

Even more troubling to Lucas the businessman was his son's refusal to take over the store he had worked so hard to build.

Chaining Himself to His Desk

Lucas, in this excerpt from Pollock's biography *Skywalking*, muses on the role of sheer hard work in his success at film school.

If it hadn't been for the self-discipline that made me chain myself to my desk and do it, my work would never have gotten done. I felt there were a lot of kids that never figured that out, and they just sort of whiled away their lives and woke up one day to find out they were thirty-five years old and hadn't amounted to much. I [realized] that a lot of the really significant things that have happened in history have come from people under the age of thirty.

George had agreed to work there during the summer, as delivery boy and general aide. But it was dull work; he was responsible, among other things, for cleaning toilets and sweeping up. After only two weeks, he not only quit but vowed never to do that sort of work for a living.

This refusal to follow George Senior's wishes led, predictably, to a blowup, one of the few times anyone can remember the normally reserved younger Lucas yelling. George Senior predicted, "You'll be back in a few years." His son shouted in reply, "I'm never coming back" and impulsively added, "I'm going to be a millionaire before I'm thirty."[17]

No one, it appears, believed in George's cocksure predictions. He had never done anything to inspire that sort of confidence. His sister Kate asserts, "George is a great inspiration for parents. Nobody would have believed he was going to do anything. He was a total loss. He's a great example for parents not to lose their cool. I'm just amazed that a person that was so untogether could turn out to be so together."[18]

Away from Home

Lucas entered USCinema as a junior. He was twenty years old, and it was his first extended stay away from home. He rented a house in the hills above Beverly Hills. The place was so dilapidated that it had no stairs; the only access between floors was an industrial ladder. Rent was only $80 per month, but even so Lucas's funds were so limited that he took in a roommate: another USC student, future *Grease* director Randal Kleiser.

Lucas had talked his father into financing his film education. Together, they worked out a deal: George Senior would "hire" his son to go to school, paying him a "salary"—that is, tuition plus expenses. For his part, Lucas was to treat school like a job, working hard and showing some return on the investment. If he failed, he agreed to return to Modesto and take over L. M. Morris . . . or else strike out on his own with no financial support.

School was tough. To be eligible to make a student film during his last year, George would have to cram two years of film studies into a single junior year. So he buckled down to work,

To afford rent during film school, George Lucas took on a roommate, fellow student Randal Kleiser, who would later direct the hit musical Grease.

surviving on a minimum of sleep and a steady diet of Hershey bars, chocolate chip cookies, and Cokes. Although drugs were popular among college students at the time, he never used them; he has always claimed it was simply because he was too busy.

Studying and writing term papers did not come easily, but Lucas heeded at least part of his father's advice: the value of sheer hard labor. He remarks of his college days that without "the self-discipline that made me chain myself to my desk and do it," he never would have graduated.[19]

"Like a Duck to Water"

Most of Lucas's fifty-odd fellow students at USCinema had been movie addicts from an early age, and were already intimately familiar with film history. They could recite minute details of dozens of movies, explain the subtle influences of one director on another, and grapple with difficult theories.

Except for what he had seen on TV, however, Lucas had never been especially drawn to movies. It took months for first-run movies to make it to Modesto's one theater, and foreign films never played there. Lucas claims, in fact, that in high school he was so indifferent to movies that he attended them only to pick up girls. The filmmaker remarks that he arrived at USC ignorant of even the most basic distinctions: "Producer and director were for me the same general category—the person who made the movies."[20]

Film school was an awakening, however, and once Lucas's eyes were opened to the possibilities of the cinema, he was a fast study. He and his fellow students would watch four or five movies every weekend, then spend hours discussing them. He saw and discussed even more films during the week in class. Quickly, Lucas formed strong, informed opinions about dozens of directors and their works.

He was especially moved by the visions of directors Stanley Kubrick, Akira Kurosawa, and Orson Welles. He loved the abstract shorts of the National Film Board of Canada. The zany editing of *A Hard Day's Night* and *Help!,* the Beatles movies directed by Richard Lester, showed him more exciting new possibilities. Journalist Garry Jenkins comments, "Thrown into a world where the heroes were [European directors] Jean-Luc Godard and Federico Fellini rather than Flash Gordon and Spiderman, Lucas was reborn. He took to filmmaking like a duck to water."[21]

"Just the Most Electrifying Things"

At first, Lucas did not stand out as a student. USCinema sound instructor Ken Mura recalls, "Basically, George was a person you really didn't notice."[22] But he was always keenly observant and absorbed his lessons quickly, notes fellow student Howard Kazanjian: "He was small, quiet, inquisitive, intelligent, witty— like a cat, eyes darting back and forth. He was trying to figure out, was this something he wanted to do? What is this business called film? What is editing, lighting, what is all of that?"[23]

As he gained self-confidence, however, Lucas's reputation grew. He discovered he had a flair for the technical areas of film-

Japanese filmmaker Akira Kurosawa received a lifetime achievement award. Kurosawa's films inspired Lucas (left) and director Steven Spielberg (right).

making, especially editing, and could work far more quickly than most of his fellow students. He became known for producing work that was not only good but completed astonishingly fast.

Lucas quickly won several awards in local student film festivals and was a legend at the school by the time he had been there a year. Every time a Lucas piece came on during a showing of student films, the excitement in the air was palpable. Fellow student Hal Robbins recalls, "His films were just the most electrifying things you had ever seen."[24]

Student Films

Students at USCinema were required to complete many filmmaking assignments, from one-minute shorts to more complex projects. Lucas's first films were unusually sophisticated for a beginning student.

For an animation class assignment to use still photos to suggest movement and action, he created *Looking at Life*, a montage about war and protesters taken from the magazine *Life*. Next came *Herbie*, which was nothing more than close-ups of a highly

Discipline

Lucas was surprised at how easily he dominated his film classes, and how quickly his skills became legendary among other students. He attributed much of this success to hard work, as shown in this passage from Pollock's *Skywalking*.

> Talent without hard work doesn't get you very far. I think the most important thing is to work very hard, and if you have the talent, it will show. You can do something by working hard—that's discipline. If you keep at it long enough, sooner or later you get lucky and get your break. But I had to work hard at acquiring the skills for filmmaking—they're all learned. After that, I had every bit of confidence when I was in film school that I was going to make it.

polished car reflecting the headlights of passing vehicles. Lucas's knack for witty editing and his eye for visual composition made these simple premises exciting.

His first longer film, made as a senior, reflected the political and social controversies of the Sixties. *Freiheit*, German for "freedom," starred his roommate Randal Kleiser as a student who tries to cross the border that then divided Germany. The attempt to escape from communist East Germany is unsuccessful, and the student is gunned down. At the end, a soldier stands over the student's body as an announcer states, "Freedom is worth dying for" and "Without freedom, we're dead."[25]

Lucas's final student film was called *1:42:08*. The movie simply follows a yellow race car as it laps around a track. (The title refers to the time length of the race.) The movie's confidence and sophistication, which made an exciting experience out of virtually nothing, took the USCinema student body by storm. Fellow student John Milius recalls, "It looked like [the] Grand Prix and everybody else was shooting some little movie on campus. There was a sense of there being no limits to what he would try."[26]

The Movie Brats

Lucas received his bachelor of arts degree in cinema in the summer of 1966. Like many film school graduates, however, he had little hope that his degree alone would get him a job in Hollywood.

Hollywood at the time was a closed world, where jobs were usually passed from one family member to another. It was nearly impossible for outsiders—especially intellectual film school graduates—to gain access to what director Orson Welles once famously called "the biggest electric train set a boy ever had." John Milius recalls, "There were walls up in Hollywood then, and the place was very clicquish. You had to know Frank Sinatra or something."[27]

At first, Lucas had no intention of storming the walls of Hollywood. He planned instead to find a job making educational or industrial films. This work, he reasoned, would provide not only financial stability but access to equipment that would allow him to make small, experimental movies for his own pleasure. This was a typical career path; Lucas recalls that the basic idea was, "You'll graduate from film school and become a ticket-taker at Disneyland, or get a job with some industrial outfit in Kansas. But nobody [from film school] had ever gotten a job in Hollywood making theatrical films."[28]

The Hollywood tradition was about to change dramatically, however. Old-style Hollywood studios generally regarded movies as interchangeable products that fell into predictable categories such as "comedy" or "drama." Under pressure from the enormous influence of television on the viewing public, however, studios were increasingly being forced to rethink their traditional ways of doing business. The long-established studio system, which produced formulaic movies with assembly-line regularity, was crumbling.

At the same time, unusually large numbers of young, gifted filmmakers were emerging from cinema schools. Unlike graduates only a few years older than George, many of these aspiring filmmakers wanted to make their way in commercial movies. They were determined to combine the old studio ways with more up-to-date ideas. In particular, they were fascinated by the *auteur* theory, the idea advanced by influential French critics that the director was the ultimate artist whose creative stamp identified him or her as the "author" of a film.

Film historians Michael Pye and Lynda Myles gave this new generation of filmmakers a label: the "movie brats." The movie brats included Lucas's group of friends at USC, which called itself the Dirty Dozen. Among them were many who would become extremely successful: future directors Robert Zemeckis, Randal Kleiser, John Milius, and John Carpenter; the writing teams of Hal Barwood/Matthew Robbins and Willard Huyck/Gloria Katz; cinematographer Caleb Deschanel; sound editor Walter Murch; and producer Howard Kazanjian.

There were other brats outside USCinema. Across town at UCLA, directors Francis Ford Coppola and Carroll Ballard were honing their skills. Just to the south at UC/Long Beach, young Steven Spielberg was proving that he already knew more than most of his teachers. And across the country, at New York University, future directors Brian de Palma and Martin Scorsese were dazzling their professors.

This new generation of filmmakers was on the verge of taking control. Over the next few years, the movie brats entered the workforce, and in time revolutionized the film industry. One of the most talented was George Lucas.

Chapter 3

American Zoetrope and *THX 1138*

Francis lives on the edge; George hugs the cliffs.
—writer Dale Pollock on the founders of American
Zoetrope, Francis Coppola and George Lucas

A company based in a beautiful place where people could work together while they enjoyed their lives and provided inspiration and advice for one another.
—Francis Coppola on the vision for American Zoetrope

LUCAS WANTED TO continue his education as a graduate film student at USC. However, by now the Vietnam War was in full swing and many young men his age were being drafted for military service.

Lucas failed the military's medical exam, however. It was discovered that he had diabetes. He immediately had to give up sugar, including his beloved Hershey bars and Cokes. Since Lucas rarely drank liquor and never smoked or used drugs, this new restriction only added to the squeaky-clean image he already had.

Marcia

By the time Lucas received his medical deferment in 1966, it was too late to start graduate school in that year. At loose ends, he found part-time work as an editor. The United States Information Agency (USIA), a government documentation group, hired him to help edit a film on President Lyndon Johnson's trip to the Far East. Soon after, the agency brought in another editor, Marcia Griffin, to help with his workload.

By coincidence, Marcia was also a native of Modesto and was about the same age as Lucas, but otherwise their backgrounds were quite different. Marcia had been raised by a single mother, and the family never had much money. Marcia began work right after high school and was a seasoned professional editor by the time she met George. This intimidated George at first, although for her part Marcia felt intellectually inferior next to the college graduate.

Despite their differences and an initial coolness toward each other, the two were attracted and soon became more than professional colleagues. She was the first woman he had ever seriously dated; going out with someone more than once or twice was a new experience for Lucas. By the spring of 1967, they were living together.

George's friends were generally surprised. The two seemed well matched in wit, intelligence, and strong will. Her outgoing nature, however, seemed at such odds to George's extreme reserve—and her good looks were, frankly, a surprise as well. John Milius recalls, "She was a knock-out. We all wondered how little George got this great-looking girl. And smart, too, obsessed with films. And she was a better editor than he was."[29]

Graduate Work and the Birth of *THX*

While still working part-time for USIA, Lucas reentered USC in the fall of 1967 as a graduate student. At USC, he created several more short films. *Anyone lived in a pretty how town* (the name comes from a poem by the eccentric American poet e.e. cummings) was a surrealistic movie about a photographer who takes pictures of a young couple and turns the people into black-and-white stills. *The Emperor* explored the idea of people having a relationship with a radio personality they have never met.

To make ends meet, Lucas was teaching a course in cinematography at USC to a group of officers from the navy's film division. Lucas recalls that working with the by-the-book military men was difficult at first: "To have this young hippie come in and teach them after they'd been at it for ten years was a challenge. But the whole idea of the class was to teach them they didn't have to go by the rule book."[30]

Lucas resolved the tension between himself and his students by creating a different sort of tension. He hit on the idea of dividing the class into two film crews. Taking half of the class as his own crew and assigning the other half to the class's ranking officer, he announced that the two teams would compete to see which could make the better film. This essentially gave Lucas a free crew with which to make a film of his own.

While he edited footage of Lyndon Johnson with Marcia during the day, by night Lucas and his navy crew filmed a darkly brooding science fiction piece, *THX 1138:4EB*. It was based on an idea he and his friend, sound editor Walter Murch, had created during their undergraduate days. It concerned one man's desperate escape from a frightening, domineering futuristic society, where the masses are kept sedated and in virtual slavery.

The message of *THX* was bleak, but the film was extremely innovative. Its use of sound-mixing and graphic techniques, such as the LED-style numbers running across the bottom of the

A New Role Model

In this excerpt from his introduction to Charles Champlin's book *George Lucas: The Creative Impulse*, Steven Spielberg recalls his first encounter with Lucas and with one of Lucas's films.

[W]e first met at a student-film festival in 1967 where the short film "THX 1138" was not yet a license plate in *American Graffiti* or a state-of-the-art sound system in a couple thousand movie theaters worldwide, but instead a vision of the future of mankind—dark and pessimistic, but nonetheless brilliantly crafted. I was jealous to the very marrow of my bones. I was eighteen years old and had directed fifteen short films by that time, and this little movie was better than all of my little movies combined. No longer were [legendary directors like] John Ford, Walt Disney, Frank Capra, Federico Fellini, David Lean, Alfred Hitchcock, or Michael Curtiz my role models. Rather, it was someone nearer my own age, someone I could actually get to know, compete with, draw inspiration from.

screen, would have been sophisticated for even a feature film. *THX* attracted serious attention, both on the student film circuit and from more mainstream observers. It won first prize in the dramatic category and honorable mentions in three other categories at that year's National Student Film Festival.

Steven Spielberg, then a film student himself, was one of the many people who were profoundly impressed by the film. When the two met, however, Spielberg recalls that Lucas did not have the same impact as his movie. Spielberg says Lucas reminded him "a little bit of Walt Disney's version of a mad scientist. He was so unassuming when I first met him that I couldn't immediately associate him with the power of *THX.*"[31]

"Francis's Life Is One Big Anecdote"

Lucas was one of four young filmmakers awarded a student scholarship to apprentice with a distinguished producer, Carl Foreman. Foreman was at work on a western called *MacKenna's Gold,* directed by the veteran J. Lee Thompson, shot in Utah and Arizona, and starring Gregory Peck, Omar Sharif, and Telly Savalas.

Each of the four students was to direct a short film about the making of *MacKenna's Gold,* with the finished versions being used as promotional trailers to advertise the movie before its release. Against Foreman's wishes, Lucas directed an abstract film about the desert. It had little to do with *MacKenna's Gold* and was virtually useless as a promotional tool. It was a beautiful little film, however, and on its strength Lucas was awarded a scholarship sponsored by the Warner Brothers studio. Lucas took a leave of absence from film school to accept the scholarship, which gave him a small amount of money and limited access to the studio's equipment and personnel.

Lucas wanted to work in the famed Warner's animation department, but it had recently closed its doors, a casualty of the general economic depression Hollywood was experiencing in the 1960s. In fact, only one feature was being shot at Warner's at the time, a lavish musical called *Finian's Rainbow.* Directing it was a recent UCLA graduate named Francis Ford Coppola. On the basis of a few quickly made features, including one for Roger

Francis Ford Coppola, around the time of Lucas and Coppola's first meeting.

Corman, the king of low-budget drive-in movies, Coppola had become one of the first movie brats to direct a Hollywood film.

When Lucas wandered over to the set and met Coppola, it was the beginning of a fruitful professional relationship and a stormy personal connection that continues to this day. "One day," Coppola recalls, "I saw a skinny young man dressed in a college sweater watching me as I worked on the set. Someone told me he was a student observer from USC. 'See anything interesting?' I asked. Slowly he shook his head, and waved his hand, palm down. 'Nope, not yet.' This is how I met George Lucas."[32]

The two very different young men were unlikely colleagues in some ways. Unlike Lucas, Coppola is burly and boisterous, a lover of personal indulgence, and tolerant of disorganization. As filmmakers, they are also a study in contrasts: Lucas always plans the smallest detail in advance, while Coppola favors improvisation and last-second changes. Lucas sums up their differences by noting dryly, "My life has no anecdotes; Francis's life is one big anecdote."[33]

Filmmaker

Despite their differences, however, the two liked each other, and Coppola took the visiting filmmaker under his wing. Coppola was only five years older than Lucas, and no one else on the *Finian's Rainbow* set was even close to them in age. Coppola was grateful for the company of someone even a little bit similar. Lucas recalls, "We were the only people on the production under forty or fifty. We had both been to film school, and we both had beards." [34]

The *Finian's Rainbow* production bored Lucas, but he stayed. He planned to spend six months at Warner's, finish his incomplete master's degree, then move to San Francisco with Marcia. His idea was to direct commercial and educational films for a living while making experimental movies on the side.

At the same time, he took up Carl Foreman's suggestion to write a story treatment (the prelude to a full-blown screenplay) that would expand *THX* into a feature-length film. Coppola

Francis Ford Coppola directing The Godfather: Part II *in 1974.*

The Seventy-Year-Old Kid

In an excerpt from Michael Pye's and Lynda Myles's book *The Movie Brats*, Lucas comments on the intense relationship he has had over the years with one of his close mentors, Francis Coppola.

We became very close friends, because in every single way we're opposite, two halves of a whole. Coppola's very impulsive and Italian and flamboyant and sort of extravagant. I'm extremely conservative and plodding. He was constantly jumping off cliffs and I was always shouting: "Don't do it, you'll get yourself killed!" He would jump anyway, and for a while nothing too bad would happen. I used to be called the seventy-year-old kid.

helped by hiring Lucas to work on *Finian* beyond the time of the apprenticeship, which provided time and money to work on the science fiction project.

Coppola then convinced a studio to pay Lucas $3,000 as an option on the story. (An option gives a studio limited rights to make a film of a story.) Lucas wanted to hire a professional writer to help him flesh out this story into a screenplay, but Coppola advised, "If you're going to make it in this business you have to learn how to write."[35]

Lucas lived on the option money while he worked without pay on Coppola's next film, *The Rain People*. He wore several hats during the cross-country production, including assistant cameraman, art director, production manager, and sound recordist. He also shot *Filmmaker*, a half-hour documentary about the production of *The Rain People*.

It was both grueling and invigorating for Lucas to be working on three projects at once. He recalls, "I'd get up at four in the morning and work on *THX* until it was time to go to work for Francis at seven. By the time we were finished looking at the dailies [daily footage shot], it was always ten or eleven at night, but I was young and it was fun."[36]

Marriage and American Zoetrope

During the *Rain People* shoot, Marcia took a break from her editing job and joined George in New York. On a train bound for a location shoot on Long Island, he proposed to her and she accepted. They were married in February 1969 in a Methodist church in Pacific Grove, California, and, after a brief honeymoon in Big Sur, they settled in a small house in Mill Valley, near San Francisco.

However, there was little editing work for Marcia locally. Reluctantly, she moved back to Los Angeles, where she edited *The Candidate* (starring a very young Robert Redford) and two early Martin Scorsese films, *Alice Doesn't Live Here Anymore* and *Taxi Driver*. The couple saw each other when they could.

Lucas's main project was in San Francisco: an ambitious scheme he and Coppola had hatched while making *The Rain People*. It was a film collective they called American Zoetrope. (A zoetrope is an antique device for displaying moving images on a wall. The Greek word *zoetrope* means "life movement," which they also felt was a fitting concept.) The studio, Zoetrope, much changed from its original form, still exists.

It was a grand, romantic plan: a community of young filmmakers, sharing equipment and ideas, operating free of the restrictions

A scene from the film Taxi Driver. *Lucas and his wife, Marcia, lived separately while she worked on this film.*

Figuring the Options

In this passage from Pollock's *Skywalking*, Marcia Lucas analyzes George's desire to separate himself from Hollywood by going to San Francisco and making avant-garde films. Marcia says she accepted this risky move because early on she had learned something about Lucas:

> Everything was a means to an end. George has always planned things very far in advance. He always works out in his head what may happen in a year or two and figures out what all the possibilities are so that he can handle whatever situation pops up. He's very good at capitalizing on all the options.

and hustle of commercial, cliquish, dollar-driven Hollywood. A press release for American Zoetrope loftily declared, "The essential objective of the company is to engage in the varied fields of film-making, collaborating with the most gifted and youthful talent using the most contemporary techniques and equipment possible." [37]

Selling *THX* and *Apocalypse Now*

Besides Coppola and Lucas, longtime Coppola associates Ron Colby and Mona Skager, as well as independent director John Korty, were involved in the collective. Using Coppola's house as collateral for a loan, the group began looking for a headquarters in the summer of 1969. Coppola also began buying expensive equipment on credit, running up huge debts with no clear plan for repayment.

The conflicts began almost immediately. Coppola's grand plan included a complete studio, state-of-the-art hardware, and such excessive amenities as helicopter pads. Lucas thought a modest house with enough space for offices and an editing studio was more appropriate. When nothing suitable could be found, they compromised on a drab warehouse in downtown San Francisco, where the group began designing and building their mini-studio on a shoestring.

Meanwhile, Coppola struck a deal with Warner Brothers to develop five scripts written by Zoetrope members. All were modeled on the hugely successful formula of the recent smash hit *Easy Rider:* low cost, modest production, high return. One possibility was *THX.* Lucas and sound editor Walter Murch, a

A rift in the friendship between Lucas and Coppola developed over the making of Apocalypse Now.

friend from USC, produced an acceptable script, and Coppola came up with a fanciful budget figure: $777,777.77. (Seven was Coppola's lucky number.)

At the same time, Lucas was working with another USC friend, John Milius, on the story of *Apocalypse Now.* Set in Vietnam, the film was envisioned as an updated version of Joseph Conrad's classic novella *Heart of Darkness.* When Warner's executives cooled on the idea of making *THX,* Coppola impulsively offered *Apocalypse Now* to the studio if they agreed to take *THX.* Warner's said yes.

Lucas agreed to write and direct *THX,* but he was shocked and angry that Coppola had even mentioned *Apocalypse Now* to the Hollywood studio. At the time Coppola had no connection to the film at all, and Lucas felt that Coppola had overstepped his bounds. Coppola's rash move got *THX* made, but it was also the beginning of a rift in the relationship, both personal and professional, between the two strong-willed filmmakers.

Shooting *THX*

Lucas was aided in the *THX* project by a good cast, including Donald Pleasance, David Ogden Stiers, and, in the lead role, Robert Duvall, who would go on to an Oscar-winning career. Overall, however, *THX* was a difficult and taxing experience for the director.

Lucas was paid only $15,000 to write and direct, and the budget for the film overall was small. His time frame for completing the work was extremely tight. Furthermore, Warner's assigned a studio line director to the project. A line producer's job is to be on the set daily, making sure a picture moves toward completion without delays or cost overruns. Lucas was angry at this show of uncertainty over his and American Zoetrope's ability to do the job unsupervised.

Since Lucas had little money and time, he carefully planned the film beforehand and used little on-set improvisation. Few retakes were needed, and occasionally Lucas was even able to shoot rehearsals and use them as prints. He also employed a local crew rather than importing one from Los Angeles. He used

THX 1138, a bleak portrayal of the future of mankind, was Lucas's first feature film.

"We Are the Pigs"

In this excerpt from Michael Pye's and Lynda Myles's *The Movie Brats,* a book about Lucas's generation of filmmakers, Lucas comments on the importance of the director in filmmaking. Until the time this generation came to prominence—the late Sixties and early Seventies—Hollywood studios had treated the director as an easily replaceable tool.

We are the pigs. We are the ones who sniff out the truffles. You can put us on a leash, keep us under control. But we are the guys who dig out the gold. The man in the executive tower cannot do that. The studios are corporations now, and the men who run them are bureaucrats. They know as much about making movies as a banker does. They know about making deals like a real estate agent. They obey corporate law; each man asks himself how any decision will affect his job. They go to parties and they hire people who know people. But the power lies with us—the ones who actually know how to make movies.

as his primary sets the Marin County Civic Center and the half-completed tunnels for the region's rapid transit system, eliminating the need for costly set construction.

The director built one miniature set himself using model parts, and found a way to use a ten-dollar fireworks assortment for one shot of explosions. Carpenter–prop man Ted Moehnke recalls of the bare-bones production, "We drove around in the van Francis Coppola used on *The Rain People,* and my prop cart was a garbage can with wheels."[38]

"A Reflex Action"

Despite Lucas's care and hard work, *THX* was, in many respects, a failure. Although it is full of striking images, the Warner's studio executives found it confusing, bleak, and depressing. After threatening to can (that is, not release) the movie, the studio executives exercised their right to make the final edit and had *THX* recut by a veteran Hollywood editor.

The final version is only a few minutes shorter than Lucas's version, but the director was furious at the studio's move. He felt the studio had arrogantly changed the film simply because it could. He says, "The ludicrous thing is that they only cut out five minutes, and it really didn't make much of a difference. I think it's just a reflex action they have."[39]

Warner's still thought *THX* was a disaster, however. Executives there were so upset that they canceled every deal they had made with Zoetrope, including *Apocalypse Now*. As a result, the collective nearly fell apart. Coppola went on an extended European vacation, bills piled up, and expensive equipment was stolen from the poorly guarded Zoetrope studios. Warner's, meanwhile, was threatening to make the unusual move of forcing Zoetrope to pay back the entire cost of producing *THX*.

In the midst of these problems, Paramount Studios asked Coppola to direct a film version of Mario Puzo's pop novel *The Godfather*. It hardly seemed like a promising project—the young filmmakers saw little chance to create art with such a commercial project—but Lucas urged Coppola to accept the job to pay off Zoetrope's mounting debts.

Meanwhile, Lucas began disassociating himself from Zoetrope. He took on a job with another filmmaking team, the Maysles brothers, shooting a documentary of a concert given by the Rolling Stones at the Altamont Speedway, near San Francisco. When *THX* was finally released in 1971, it bombed, just as Warner's had predicted. Even after it was rereleased in the wake of *Star Wars*'s success, with the extra minutes reinstated, *THX* remains one of Lucas's rare commercial failures.

With his first studio movie, Lucas had gone from whiz kid film student to box office poison. The director, mindful of the Hollywood cliché that "you're only as good as your last picture," knew that a warmer, more commercial film could rescue his reputation. Francis Coppola remarks, "I think George was traumatized by *THX* and realized that his career was going to be dependent on how accessible people found his work."[40]

Fortunately, Lucas had a couple of good ideas, and one of them took him back to his Modesto roots.

Chapter 4

American Graffiti

*It's a significant event in the maturation of American youth. It's
a rite of passage [and] so American.*
　　　　　　—George Lucas on car cruising

*"Guerrilla filmmaking" is the only way to describe it. It was
like "run up on the porch and get the scene before the owner gets
home!"*
　　　　　　—Richard Dreyfuss on the filming of *American Graffiti*

Looking back to his cruising days, Lucas began planning a
film that would take in several interwoven stories bound together by a sound track of songs and the radio disc jockey who
was playing the tunes. The music would be as important as the
stories or the characters. "All through the film," sound editor
Walter Murch recalls of Lucas's concept, "people would be
swimming in a soup of sound."[41]

Dealmaking

While making *THX*, Lucas told his USC friends, the husband-and-
wife writing team of Willard Huyck and Gloria Katz, "I have an idea
I'd love you guys to do. It's a rock 'n' roll movie and it takes place
in the 50s and it's about cruising and music and deejays."[42]

Lucas, Huyck, and Katz wrote an eight-page story treatment
around the idea, and Lucas's agent began shopping it to studios.
Then, in the spring of 1970, the Lucases attended the annual
Cannes Film Festival in the south of France. Even though they
had almost no money, they decided to continue their European
jaunt with backpacks and sleeping bags.

In London for his twenty-sixth birthday, Lucas got a call from a top executive at United Artists: the studio liked *American Graffiti*. UA agreed to pay Lucas for a full-length screenplay. Unfortunately, Huyck and Katz had to pass, because they had committed to another project. Lucas asked Gary Kurtz, a producer he had contacted to help with the project, to quickly hire another screenwriter. Lucas hated the results, however, finding the writer's approach too crude.

Punching It Up

Unfortunately, Kurtz had given the writer all the available money. The funds were gone, and Lucas still lacked a screenplay. He tried rewriting *Graffiti* himself, but the studio rejected his version.

By now he was in debt to his family and friends, and the outlook was grim. Lucas had been the first of his USC group to have made a feature—and now it seemed as though he might never get a second chance.

Still, Lucas resisted the temptation of easy money to stay with his idea. Although offered $100,000 to direct *Lady Ice*, a caper movie with Donald Sutherland, he didn't like the script and turned it down. *Lady Ice* was eventually made, with dismal results; Lucas remarks, "My career would have been ruined if I'd done it; that would have been the end of me." [43]

Fortunately, Huyck and Katz were able to rejoin the rock 'n' roll project. Lucas and the writers spent two weeks generating ideas by talking about things that had happened to them in high school.

More Hard Work

In this passage from Pollock's *Skywalking*, Lucas outlines the strenuous schedule necessary in making a movie.

When you're directing, you have to get up at four thirty, have breakfast at five, leave the hotel at six, drive an hour to location, start shooting at eight, and finish shooting around six. Then you wrap, go to your office, and set up the next day's work. You get back to the hotel about eight or nine, hopefully get a bite to eat, then you go to your room and figure out your homework, how you're going to shoot the next day's scenes, and then you go to sleep. The next morning it starts all over again.

The results were excellent. Lucas says of the developed characters, "They were cardboard cutouts in my script, nonpeople. Bill and Gloria made it one hundred percent better with a combination of wit, charm, snappy one-liners, and punched-up characters."[44]

$15 a Week More

By this time, however, UA executives had lost interest in the project. A new studio, Universal, entered the picture. Universal approved the movie and gave it a budget of $750,000, a modest figure even then. This amount had to cover everything, including Lucas's $50,000 director's fee and fees for the rights to use the crucial sound track music.

Lucas wanted Kurtz to be the movie's producer, but Universal insisted on a bigger name. *The Godfather* had just opened, to ecstatic critical acclaim and enormous box office profits; Francis Coppola had made a brilliant work of art out of Puzo's novel, and the director was the hottest thing in

To save the failing American Zoetrope, Coppola directed The Godfather, *a film that catapulted him to fame.*

Hollywood. Lucas recalls, "Universal said that, if Francis would put his name on the film, they would give it the go-ahead." [45]

Coppola and Kurtz agreed to act as coproducers. Lucas knew that Coppola was primarily just lending his name; Kurtz was the one who would be on the set every day, making sure everything ran on schedule and within budget. A company was established: Lucasfilms, Ltd. was jointly owned by Marcia and George Lucas, with Gary Kurtz and a secretary, Bunny Alsup, as its only employees.

Fred Roos, a longtime Coppola associate, was hired to oversee the casting process, with remarkable results: *Graffiti*'s roster of performers may include more then-unknown future stars than any other movie in history. Among them: Richard Dreyfuss, Harrison Ford, Ron Howard, Cindy Williams, Suzanne Somers, Candy Clark, Charles Martin Smith, Kay Lenz, Paul LeMat, and Mackenzie Phillips.

While Ron Howard had been a child actor on television, he had never been cast in an adult role; none of the other faces was familiar. Harrison Ford had been making a living as a carpenter, with only occasional acting jobs. He recalls of his audition for *Graffiti*, "I was making twice as much [as a carpenter] as they were offering me to be in the movie. So I refused at first. But when they called back with an offer of $15 a week more, I took it." [46]

Problems

Shooting on *Graffiti* began in June 1972, on a tight schedule of less than a month. Lucas's home town of Modesto had grown too big to have the authentic feel the director wanted, so he used the small town of San Rafael, in Marin County.

The production had its share of disasters. San Rafael had agreed, for a fee, to let Lucas use its main thoroughfare at night. On the second night of shooting, however, the town revoked the license. A bar owner, complaining of blocked access, was threatening to sue. A production assistant hastily found another location, in nearby Petaluma, but a precious few days had been lost.

The time constraints were so great that Lucas asked his friend, cinematographer Haskell Wexler, to come from Los Angeles at the last moment to relieve some of the production

Improvising on the Set

In Pollock's book *Skywalking*, Lucas admits that with more time and money he could have made *Graffiti* a more polished film. A director, however, must improvise according to the problems that occur daily.

It's what's on the screen that counts. The job in film is to do the impossible every day, and you get thrown things from left field all the time. The job of the director is to go with the punches—you just keep doing it until the film is finished.

And in Champlin's *George Lucas: The Creative Impulse*, Harrison Ford recalls how the stress of constant improvising during the filming of *Graffiti* on a shoestring budget affected its director:

George was under incredible strain. He was working his tail to the bone. It was such a low cost production that we didn't have a camera car, for example. What we did was haul one picture car with another picture car on a trailer we'd rented from U-Haul. Then we took the trunk lid off the lead car so the sound man, the cameraman, and George could crouch in the trunk.

I remember a scene where we had to circle the block again and again and again. Afterward, we went up to the camera car to see how it had gone, and George had fallen asleep in the trunk.

pressure. Though he already had a hectic daily schedule, Wexler flew to Marin every evening to create the movie's distinctively garish, neon-seeming lighting.

Like virtually everyone else on the production, Coppola was amazed by Lucas's breakneck speed. He complained good-naturedly, "I go to great lengths to get interesting compositions for *The Godfather*, and the kid here comes over, sets up the camera, puts everybody up against the wall, and just shoots."[47]

Way Too Few Doughnuts

Graffiti's action takes place during a single long night, so nearly all its filming took place between 9 P.M. and 5 A.M. Lucas, not a night owl, had to adapt to a grueling all-night schedule, and the director, never robust, developed various physical woes as the pressure mounted. He suffered nearly constant headaches, nausea, and coldlike symptoms during the shoot. He was tired so much of the time he occasionally dozed off during a shot.

There were other problems as well. On one occasion, an assistant cameraman was accidentally struck by a car. The crew member was not seriously hurt, but the incident upset everyone. Another near disaster occurred as Lucas shot the film's climactic crash scene: two cameramen were nearly killed when a car failed to veer away as planned. Not all the problems *Graffiti*'s crew and cast had to deal with were serious. Harrison Ford says his main memories of the film's shooting are "very little time, very little money, and very few doughnuts. I almost got fired for taking more than my share of doughnuts."[48]

Despite the problems plaguing the shoot, the high-spirited group of young actors on the set formed a close bond, acting as though they were at summer camp. One night, according to legend, Harrison Ford led an expedition to climb to the top of the sign outside their motel. Another story has Ford and LeMat throwing Dreyfuss out a second-story window into a swimming pool. Casting director Roos recalls, "It was a giddy time."[49]

Postproduction

The production wrapped in August 1972. Next came the complicated process of postproduction, when rough footage was edited and sound effects added.

Lucas's original idea had been to use eighty songs in the all-important sound track. However, the costs of licensing so much music proved prohibitive. Universal's executives, not understanding how crucial the music was to the movie's overall effect, wanted to cut the number to five or six. A compromise of forty-five songs was

Actor Harrison Ford starred in several George Lucas films.

reached. Unfortunately, no music by one of the era's most important singers, Lucas's beloved Elvis Presley, could be included; the Presley estate wanted too much money.

Throughout the entire production and postproduction process, there was little feeling that *Graffiti* would be a major film. Few expected this minor little movie about a bunch of kids to be more than a forgettable drive-in film, and certainly no one thought it would ever be considered deep or meaningful. As Harrison Ford dryly puts it, "There was an understanding that what were called 'youth films' had not represented the experience of young people. I mean, *Beach Blanket Bingo* was not really a revelation about the mysteries of life."[50]

Preview

At *Graffiti's* first sneak preview, held on a Sunday morning in January 1973 at a small theater in San Francisco, the audience of eight hundred loved the film; they cheered, shouted, laughed, and applauded throughout. But a Universal executive in attendance, Ned Tanen, announced afterward that it was unreleasable. What happened next is the stuff of Hollywood legend.

Kurtz, Lucas, Coppola, and the others involved were stunned. Coppola loudly lectured Tanen, insisting that Lucas had produced a hit—and that Universal should be eternally grateful. Coppola claims that he offered to buy the film on the spot if Universal didn't want it. Tanen disputes this version, saying that he simply wanted only small changes and got into a shouting match with Coppola, whom he calls a bully.

In any event, Tanen insisted on making a few changes, as was the studio's right, despite Lucas's opposition. Only four and a half minutes were cut, including a scene where Harrison Ford sings "Some Enchanted Evening" to his date. However, in a film with multiple stories as tightly interwoven as those in *Graffiti*, even those small cuts were crucial to the story's continuity and flow.

Besides, to Lucas the situation was just like Warner's gratuitous cuts in *THX*. It offended the filmmaker's sense of right and wrong, of justice, that he had inherited from his stern father, and it added to his already strong disdain of Hollywood executives.

He complains, "They were simply coming in and putting a crayon mark on my painting and saying, 'Hey, don't worry about it. It's just a crayon mark.'"[51]

Surprise Hit

At the next preview, in Los Angeles in May, audience reaction was as before: the viewers loved the film. Tanen says that he packed the screening with enthusiastic teens to convince his fellow executives, who thought *Graffiti* was undoubtedly a bomb, that instead it would be a hit: "Universal was trying to get rid of it, and I set up a screening. I called Wolfman Jack [the legendary disc jockey who plays himself in the movie] and said, 'Get me 500 crazy kids tonight.' And then I prevailed on the people at Universal to come. As soon as the logo came on and the music began, the kids started dancing and yelling and that was the end of everything. It woke everybody up."[52]

Wolfman Jack, the legendary radio personality, plays himself in the film American Graffiti.

The film opened in New York and Los Angeles in August 1973. It did not "open big," setting new records, but unlike most movies it was steadily popular everywhere: in small towns and big cities, in the Midwest as well as on both coasts. Clearly, the movie—and its director—had touched a responsive chord in the American public. Solid word-of-mouth advertising also gave the film remarkable "legs": that is, it had long-lasting popularity beyond its initial opening. *Graffiti* played nonstop for nearly a year at some theaters. Journalist Peter Bart writes, "*Graffiti* did unspectacular business at first, but kept building, week after week, until it emerged as that year's major sleeper."[53]

Lucas was hurt when the San Francisco *Chronicle* panned the film. The *Chronicle* was the only paper his family read, and he knew that they would get a bad impression. However, most reviewers loved it; typical was the *Los Angeles Times* critic, who wrote, "One of the most important films of the year, as well as the one most likely to move you to tears."[54]

At the 1973 Academy Awards ceremony, *Graffiti* was nominated for five Oscars: best picture, best director, best original screenplay, best supporting actress (Candy Clark), and best editing. However, the ceremony was swept that year by *The Sting*, a caper movie starring Robert Redford and Paul Newman, and *Graffiti* did not win anything. Although he publicly claimed not to care, many observers say that Lucas was unhappy that the movie was passed over. However, most of the young, unknown cast and crew were thrilled just to get attention for what they had thought was a throwaway movie.

The Money Rolls In

Graffiti eventually became, almost certainly, the single most profitable investment ever made by a Hollywood studio. It cost only $775,000 to make (plus another $500,000 for prints, advertisements, and publicity), but it took in a whopping $117 million. On a cost-to-income scale, *Graffiti* remains by far the most profitable of all of Lucas's films.

When *Graffiti* was released, the Lucases were not only broke; they were in debt. Following the movie's release, however, they had about $4 million after taxes. Two years ahead of schedule, twenty-eight-year-old Lucas had fulfilled his rash prophecy of becoming a millionaire.

Lucas proudly repaid his father and others he had borrowed from. Most of the remaining money went into conservative investments such as land, municipal bonds, and savings accounts. Lucasfilms hired a bookkeeper. The Lucases also bought a house for themselves in San Rafael, and another nearby to serve as Lucasfilms's offices. Among Lucas's few personal indulgences were a used Ferrari and an investment in a New York City comic-book store.

But Lucas also did something nearly unheard of in the cutthroat world of moviemaking: he shared the wealth. Lucas gave new cars to people who had been key in *Graffiti*'s success, plus thousands of dollars in cash and gifts to other crew members. Points (percentages of the film's net profits, paid in a similar way to royalties) were awarded to Huyck and Katz, Kurtz,

"If You Hate It That Much, Let It Go"

While most of the preview audience loved *American Graffiti*, conservative Universal studio executives threatened to block distribution. Here are two versions of how studio executive Ned Tanen was persuaded to back down on the threat to can the movie. The first is Tanen's reaction (reprinted from Pollock's *Skywalking*) and the second is Coppola's version (excerpted from Peter Biskind's *Easy Riders, Raging Bulls*).

TANEN: My reaction was, "This is a terrific movie. But there are a couple of problems, and here it goes on too long." Things of that nature. I had an unpleasant conversation with Francis. . . . He just became very belligerent, and I became very belligerent. I'll take half the blame. I don't deal well with bullies, and it got a little unpleasant. But not with George. He was at the other end of the theater.

COPPOLA: You should go down on your knees and thank George for saving your job. This kid has killed himself to make this movie for you. He brought it in on time and on schedule. The least you can do is thank him for that. . . . If you hate it that much, let it go, we'll set it up someplace else, and get you all your money back.

Lucas's lawyer, and cinematographer Wexler, who had worked without a salary.

Another point was split between the principal cast members, and the actors saw their modest salaries dwarfed by this gift, which amounted to over $50,000 each. Ron Howard recalls, "It was a totally and completely uncommon act. I don't know if anyone's ever done anything quite like that. . . . [I]t was such a wonderfully gracious thing to do."[55]

Next Stop: Space

In the wake of *Graffiti*'s success, Lucas began pondering his next move. One possibility was *Apocalypse Now*. In 1974, after years of wrangling back and forth over the movie's fate, Francis Coppola suggested that they make it quickly. He was convinced that if it was released in 1976, America's bicentennial year, the film would have a huge impact. Coppola wanted to produce it, with Lucas directing.

Lucas, however, had just closed a deal with 20th Century-Fox for a new film. He still wanted to direct *Apocalypse Now*, and asked Coppola to wait; but Coppola insisted that an immediate start was essential. When Coppola proposed to direct the Vietnam film himself, Lucas, tired of the bickering, wearily agreed.

The new project Lucas was by now immersed in was an ambitious and unlikely science fiction saga. It was, at that point, entitled *The Star Wars*.

Chapter 5

Star Wars

George talked about buying Flash Gordon *[but] the people who owned the rights wouldn't sell it to him. So he just thought, "I'll go off and create my own thing."*
—Francis Coppola

George is not intimidated by risk. And when the risk pays off, I think it empowers him to do it again.
—Steven Spielberg

Making *American Graffiti* exhausted Lucas, and he was disgusted with the fight over Universal's cutting of the film. He was ready to quit directing, and now he could afford to retire.

However, he had been working off and on for several years on his space saga, and the chance to make *Star Wars* (as it was eventually retitled) proved irresistible.

Influences

From the beginning, Lucas envisioned *Star Wars* as a deeply personal statement that brought together many of his most closely held beliefs and ideas. At the same time, the filmmaker was determined to make it easily accessible entertainment, and he sensed that a return to the classic action-adventure form would be a hit.

For some of his inspiration, Lucas drew on the emotional impact of the westerns, sci-fi movies, and cliff-hangers he'd loved as a boy. For deeper philosophical elements, Lucas extensively studied fairy tales, myths, folklore, and religions from around the world. He was especially influenced by Joseph Campbell's scholarly books on mythology and by Carlos Castaneda's books about a mystical teacher, Don Juan.

He also incorporated his own beliefs, such as his feelings about responsibility and morality. These were basic values that had been drummed into him as a boy, when he had begun to understand the importance of self-sacrifice, persistence, and a commitment to a higher purpose. These themes, Lucas points out, are universal and ancient:

> Star Wars has always struck a chord with people. There are issues of loyalty, of friendship, of good and evil. The themes came from stories and ideas that have been around for thousands of years. . . . I mean, there's a reason this film is so popular. It's not that I'm giving out propaganda nobody wants to hear.[56]

Selling and Negotiating

Lucas was and remains an agonizingly slow writer, and the concepts in his head take shape on paper only after long periods of incubation. Even when he completed his story treatment of the original *Star Wars*, no one understood it; the first sentence announced that it was "the story of Mace Windu, a revered Jedi-bendu of Opuchi who was related to Usby C. J. Thape, padawaan learner of the famed Jedi."[57]

The universe Lucas envisioned clearly in his imagination failed to come alive even when he described it enthusiastically to friends. Gloria Katz recalls, "George acted out *Star Wars*—the whole movie—on the floor of our house. We thought he was out of his mind. I didn't get it. He was talking about Chewbacca and Jedi Bandu. We were like, 'What?!'"[58]

Lucas's agent and lawyer were equally bewildered, but agreed to help him sell the idea. Before *Graffiti* opened, when Lucas was still a high-risk director, the *Star Wars* story he had been developing was turned down by both studios he had worked with, United Artists and Universal. However, 20th Century-Fox executive Alan Ladd Jr. offered Lucas $15,000 to develop a draft script. Noting that this modest deal with the Fox studio took place just before *Graffiti* became a hit, Lucas recalls,

"That was a big deal to me then, because it meant I could pay off my debts and survive for the rest of the year."[59]

"It'll Be Fun"

Shortly after *Graffiti* opened, Ladd offered Lucas $50,000 to write a final screenplay and $100,000 to direct. Lucas was now the hottest young filmmaker in Hollywood and his agent wanted to negotiate more money. However, Lucas declined. Instead, he asked for forty percent of the movie's net profits and guarantees that he would control the film's final cut, all rights over sequels, and any merchandising.

These requests, Lucas insists, were based more on power than on money. He had always seen *Star Wars* as a nine-part saga, and he wanted to control the quality of sequels. He also thought that *Star Wars* dolls and other merchandise might be popular, and he wanted to ensure their quality as well.

The Fox lawyers were happy to give Lucas most of the guarantees he asked for. The studio still wanted control over the final cut (though they never exercised this right); but to Fox the questions of merchandising and sequels were throwaways, called "garbage" provisions. No one suspected that these provisions would be Lucas's ticket to launching the vast financial empire he controls today.

No one, in fact, expected the movie to be a big success—least of all its creator. Lucas recalls, "I thought it was too wacky for the general public. I just said, 'Well, I've had my big hit [with *Graffiti*], and I'm happy. And I'm going to do this kind of crazy thing, and it'll be fun, and that will be that.'"[60]

Dragging the Story Out

As with the story treatment, writing the script for *Star Wars* was slow going. When especially frustrated, Lucas had a habit of snipping off bits of his hair with scissors; his secretary gauged the intensity of the filmmaker's writing sessions by how much hair was in the wastebasket the next day. Lucas says of each sentence, "They get dragged out kicking and screaming with a lot of pain."[61]

He worked (as he still does) in longhand, writing in tiny print on special blue-and-green-lined paper. He used only No. 2 pencils, and his secretary would type up pages as he finished them. His notoriously poor spelling (he might spell a name several different ways on a single page) made it even more difficult for her to decipher the material.

Millions of fans are familiar with the movie's plot, in which rebel forces battle an oppressive empire and a young man, Luke Skywalker, becomes a Jedi knight. The early drafts of Lucas's screenplay, however, bear little resemblance to the final version. For instance, the hero was originally an elderly Jedi knight, not young Skywalker. At one stage, a twelve-year-old Princess Leia was the main character.

Obi-Wan Kenobi and Darth Vader, who represent the light and dark sides of the mysterious power known as the Force, were originally conceived of as the same person. Luke Skywalker was called Luke Starkiller until the last moment. In early drafts, the raffish space pirate Han Solo made only a brief appearance, as a huge, green-skinned alien with gills.

Director George Lucas (right) with Sir Alec Guinness, who played Obi-Wan Kenobi, on the set of Star Wars.

Lucas and the cast of Star Wars *in January 1997 at a viewing of* Star
Wars: Special Edition.

Nonetheless, Lucas's basic vision of what he wanted remained
true. Alan Ladd Jr. remarks, "George had many permutations on
the picture. He once thought of it with an all-Japanese cast. . . . But
it was always clear to me what he was going to do." [62]

His Own Money

When finally done, Lucas's enormous script was long enough
for three movies. Willard Huyck and Gloria Katz helped him di-
vide it into separate sections, and also helped him improve the
weak dialogue.

After Lucas delivered his script, some skeptical Fox executives were still uncertain whether to proceed. Impatient to get
started, he used some of his own money to start preproduction,
the steps before actual shooting on a film. A major part of this
was the casting process.

Resisting the studio's desire to use big-name stars, Lucas
sought offbeat choices. He considered Toshiro Mifune, famous for

his roles in Japanese samurai epics, for the part of Obi-Wan Kenobi. Other actors considered included Christopher Walken and Richard Dreyfuss as Han Solo, Robert Englund (later Freddie of *Nightmare on Elm Street* fame) as Luke, and Amy Irving and Jodie Foster as Princess Leia. Eventually, Harrison Ford joined Carrie Fisher and Mark Hamill in the primary roles, with the distinguished British actor Sir Alec Guinness as Obi-Wan Kenobi.

Besides casting, another aspect of preproduction involves finding sound stages and locations. *Star Wars* was going to require more stages than would be available in Hollywood, so producer Gary Kurtz located Elstree Studios outside London. Elstree was also a prudent choice because English crews worked for less money than American crews. In addition, Kurtz and Lucas chose Tunisia for the exterior scenes set on Luke's desert home planet, Tatooine.

Special effects, meanwhile, would be handled by a firm Lucas formed for the occasion, Industrial Light & Magic. Hiring people and finding suitable hardware was difficult; in the mid-1970s, relatively few effects artists worked in Hollywood, and available equipment was crude by today's standards. Jim Nelson, one of the company's first directors, recalls of ILM's original location, "There were four walls, no rooms, even. We had to build rooms, buy equipment, make equipment, because the equipment that made that film didn't exist."[63]

Shooting Begins

By the time Fox approved the picture, late in 1975, Lucas had spent almost a million dollars of his own money. Lucas wanted a budget of $12 million for the movie, but when the studio objected they compromised on $8.5 million (a figure that later grew to $10 million). Shooting finally began in March 1976. Fox hoped to release the movie by Christmas—but that was before the endless problems began.

The Tunisian desert was bitter cold at night and broiling hot during the day. Many crew and cast members suffered from dysentery, a serious gastrointestinal disease. Sandstorms clogged the equipment and pitted camera lenses. An especially fierce storm destroyed the sandcrawler, the vehicle used in the film by

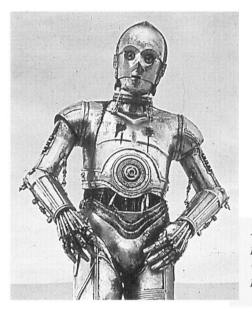

Anthony Daniels, who played the part of C3PO, lost four pounds a day in perspiration from the fierce Tunisian heat.

the beady-eyed alien characters called Jawas. In addition, Kenny Baker, the 3-foot, 8-inch actor inside R2-D2's shell, couldn't hear the director over his radio, only Tunisian stations; a crew member had to hit the shell with a hammer to stop Baker from continuing to move when a scene was over.

Anthony Daniels, the British actor who played C3PO, had his own special woes. It took a minimum of two hours every day to fit him into his tight fiberglass costume, which he then had to wear in the desert heat. He lost an average of four pounds a day through perspiration, and could not eat, drink, or use the bathroom without the aid of a helper. It was, he says, "like living in a biscuit tin [cookie jar] with no human contact—a kind of deprivation torture."[64]

England

Conditions were even worse in England. The house the Lucases rented was burglarized, they disliked British food, and Marcia came down with the flu. It was also the hottest English summer in years, and everyone was miserable under the bright set lights. Once Peter Mayhew, the 7-foot, 2-inch actor playing Chewbacca, collapsed in his heavy suit from heat exhaustion.

Adding to the unpleasantness was the British crew's open ridicule. They made fun of the strange sets and characters, and they resented the young American director's remote manner and inability to explain what he wanted. The final insult came when the crew took advantage of a British custom and declined to work overtime. Lucas's tight schedule was squeezed even tighter, and he was forced to bicycle frantically between the spread-apart sets, trying to pack as much as possible into a given day. Not surprisingly, he suffered constant head and stomach pains. (Following this rocky start, Lucas resolved his problems with filming in England, and *Star Wars* productions have since enjoyed a much better reception from crews there.)

Unlike the crew, the cast had a good time. David Prowse, a 6-foot, 7-inch weightlifter and actor, loved to stride around the set in his Darth Vader costume. As Harrison Ford recalls, "The only damper on the pure fun of that set was the almost-unanimous attitude of the English crew that we were totally out of our minds, especially George."[65]

"Oh, Another First!"

Lucas's heavy workload did not lighten up when he returned to America. He spent half his work week at home helping Marcia and her colleagues, Richard Chew and Paul Hirsch, with the film's rough editing, and the rest at ILM in Los Angeles overseeing the special-effects work.

Though *Star Wars*'s effects may seem crude by today's standards, they were state of the art in the 1970s. Furthermore, they were created on a tiny budget. Mark Hamill recalls, "I remember George saying, 'This is the most expensive low-budget film ever made.' [The spirit of the filmmaking] had a breeziness and a freedom that we never had again."[66]

During the course of the project, the ILM crew created many techniques and tools that are now standard. One of the most important of these was the Dykstraflex, a computer-controlled camera that can film a stationary model over and over, in a series of precisely calibrated passes. This allowed effects artists to build natural-looking multiple effects on a single piece of film.

Breakthroughs like the Dykstraflex came at a price, however.

The Opening Shot

Richard Edlund, one of the lead special-effects artists on *Star Wars*, recalls (in this passage from Pollock's *Skywalking*) that the opening shot of the looming, seemingly endless *Star Destroyer* could make or break the movie.

> If somebody sat down in a theater and saw this monstrous thing come over the screen and keep coming and coming, and they were awed by that, then we had our audience just where we wanted 'em. But if they laughed, we were dead.

Sixty-hour weeks were the norm, and summer temperatures at ILM's warehouse facility reached as much as 115 degrees. The crew generally worked at night, when the thermometer dipped to 90.

Furthermore, effects chief John Dykstra ran through his $3 million budget without producing any finished footage. Furious, Lucas fired Dykstra and had to change many of his planned shots: "I had to cut corners like crazy. . . . I cut out over one hundred special effects shots. The film is about 25 percent of what I wanted it to be."[67]

Despite the pressure, spirits at ILM were high. The crew—almost one hundred people, with an average age of only twenty-seven—was innovative and energetic in solving the film's many impossible-seeming technical problems. Effects artist Richard Edlund recalls the almost daily innovations: "Some guy across the stage would say, 'Oh, another first!' Some other new thing had been done that we knew hadn't been done before."[68]

Previews

As problems mounted, the production fell far behind schedule. Fox scrapped the planned Christmas release and set a new date for the summer of 1977. At several points, nervous studio executives threatened to close the project down and cut their losses. However, Lucas and Alan Ladd, his loyal ally at Fox, stubbornly succeeded in keeping it afloat.

When Lucas showed a rough cut to a group of friends, most were skeptical about its potential success. Brian de Palma was openly scornful, teasing Lucas about "those pastries" on Princess

Leia's head. Even Lucas was not sure the film would amount to anything. One of the few who felt upbeat about it was Steven Spielberg, who said, "George, it's great. It's gonna make $100 million."[69]

The reaction at the first previews was as positive as Spielberg's. Audiences began cheering when they saw the now-famous opening shot of the enormous Empire spaceship—and the cheering didn't stop. A screening for the cast and crew was just as electrifying; after months of work on isolated, baffling shots, Richard Edlund recalls, suddenly everything made sense: "We all sat there with our mouths open, and all you could hear throughout the audience was '*Wowww!*'"[70]

As the opening date drew near, producer Gary Kurtz and Fox's ad director helped fire up excitement among science fiction fans. They made the rounds of sci-fi conferences, speaking and passing out buttons and posters with the legend "*Star Wars: Coming to your galaxy soon.*" Otherwise, there was little advance publicity for the movie, partly because it was still being edited and effects were still being added. No one at Fox knew exactly what shape *Star Wars* would finally take.

"Send Money"

The film opened in only thirty-two theaters around the country in May 1977. According to some sources, the number was small because theaters were carefully selected for high-quality sound and picture presentation. Other observers maintain that only a handful of theaters were willing to take a chance on a dubious-sounding science fiction fantasy.

In any event, on opening night theater owners were astonished to find long lines forming outside their venues hours before doors opened. The word had spread from sci-fi fans to the general public: this was going to be special.

Lucas was apparently so preoccupied with finishing foreign-language versions of his movie that he forgot the date of the Los Angeles opening. He met Marcia for dinner at a hamburger restaurant near a Hollywood landmark, Grauman's Chinese Theater. As they ate, they noticed an immense traffic jam and crowds around the theater, but it wasn't until later that they realized what the commotion was about: *Star Wars.*

A crowd forms outside a New York City movie theater, awaiting the start of Star Wars.

The next day, the Lucases flew to Hawaii for their first vacation in years, accompanied by Steven Spielberg and several other friends. Despite the effort to distance himself from opening-weekend jitters, Lucas received a call from the Fox marketing head with astonishing news: *Star Wars's* opening had taken in more money per theater than any film in history.

When he returned, Lucas was greeted by thousands of fan letters and congratulatory messages. One wry telegram read, in its entirety, "Send money. Francis."[71]

A Cultural Phenomenon

The astonishing figures kept arriving. By July, *Star Wars* recouped its expenses. It passed another milestone, earning a gross income of $100 million, faster than any picture in history. By the end of the summer, the movie had raked in $134 million domestically. And in November, *Star Wars* bested Spielberg's blockbuster *Jaws* as the biggest moneymaker in history.

Star Wars became more than a gigantic money earner; it turned into a unique news event and a genuine sociological phenomenon. It also began selling millions of dollars' worth of items other than movie tickets.

The sound track album of John Williams's stirring score was a huge seller. *Star Wars* characters appeared in dozens of forms, from bubble gum to dolls and pajamas, from Princess Leia underwear to Darth Vader telephones. A novelization of the film, ghost-written under Lucas's name, shot to number one on the best-seller lists; some two dozen *Star Wars*–related novels, expanding and deepening the story line, would later appear.

Star Wars quickly became the most lucrative franchise in Hollywood history. However, Lucas decreed that its characters could not be used to advertise anything but the movie itself. Exceptions were allowed for *Sesame Street*, the children's television show, and a few public-service appearances.

As the money rolled in, Lucas again shared the wealth. Although accounts vary with respect to specifics, *Star Wars* made several people besides Lucas into millionaires.

No More Heavyweight Bouts

Star Wars was a hit with many critics, and at that year's Academy Awards ceremony it was nominated for ten Oscars, including best director, best picture, and best screenplay. Lucas claimed he did not want to attend the ceremony. However, he agreed to go with Marcia because she and her colleagues had been nominated for an editing award.

The editing team did win, and the movie won four other Oscars in technical categories. In addition, a special award went to audio engineer Ben Burtt for his innovative sound effects. But *Star Wars* won no major awards, such as best director or best picture. Although Lucas claimed to be indifferent, many observers again noted that the director seemed disappointed.

As with *American Graffiti*, Lucas had taken an enormous risk, overcome daunting obstacles, and scored a triumphant victory. There was a cost: midway through the movie's production, he had been briefly hospitalized for hypertension and exhaustion. He compared directing to "fighting a fifteen-round heavyweight bout with a new opponent every day"[72] and swore he would never do it again. Instead Lucas began what he ironically referred to as his retirement.

Chapter 6

Life After *Star Wars*

Special-effects movies are hard on actors. You find yourself giving an impassioned speech to a big lobster in a flight suit.
—Mark Hamill

Come on. They're only movies.
—George Lucas

THE RUNAWAY SUCCESS of *Star Wars* took everyone by surprise and convinced Lucas of the need to finish the story he'd begun. He already had the screenplays for the two sequels, *The Empire Strikes Back* and *Return of the Jedi;* they were the unfilmed two-thirds of his original script. True to his vow to quit directing, though, he wanted to step back to the less stressful position of producer. His newfound wealth allowed him to finance the project himself, without having to rely on a studio.

More American Graffiti

Before he could go ahead, however, Lucas had to oversee a different sequel. According to his contract with Universal, Lucas owed the studio another movie. Universal, predictably, wanted a continuation of the enormously successful *American Graffiti.*

Lucas was not interested in directing or writing; he felt the story was finished. At the same time, he did not want his carefully developed characters used clumsily or without his supervision.

As a compromise, Lucas developed the basic story and acted as executive producer for the sequel, *More American Graffiti.* Howard Kazanjian, Lucas's USC classmate, was the line producer, overseeing the film's day-to-day operation, and a young but experienced filmmaker, Bill Norton, was hired to write and direct.

Lucas's story brought the *Graffiti* characters into the next decade, the turbulent 1960s. He decided to shoot the film's separate story lines in distinctly different styles and formats, emphasizing the jittery nature of the time period. Lucas says, "I thought the fragmented technique would be a good way to tell a story about the 60s."[73]

When the movie was released in 1979, however, it was a box office disappointment, barely making back the $6 million budget that had gone into the production. While audiences had been charmed by the original's nostalgic look at a relatively innocent era, few wanted to see a gritty, pessimistic portrayal of a time characterized by drugs, war, and free love.

Empire Takes Shape

A far more promising project was the next *Star Wars* movie. To direct *The Empire Strikes Back*, Lucas selected a Hollywood veteran, Irvin Kershner. Producer Gary Kurtz and editor Paul Hirsch were only two of the many crew members returning from the first film.

Also returning were all the principal actors—though for substantially more money, since they were now celebrities. Sensitive to criticism that *Star Wars* had an all-white cast, Lucas

"Am I Still in This Movie?"

According to legend, Lucas's direction primarily consists of the phrases "Faster, more intense" and "That was great, let's do it again." In this passage from Garry Jenkins's book *Empire Building*, producer and longtime Lucas associate Gary Kurtz explains that this unwillingness to deal with actors was one reason for Lucas's retirement from directing.

All the actors complained . . . that they were concerned they were doing all right, because George never talked to them. I remember Richard Dreyfuss asking George [while shooting *American Graffiti*], "Am I still in this movie?" All actors are insecure and they need the feedback. A big chunk of a director's job is to be there and help with that. That's one of the reasons why George gave up directing. He doesn't like interacting with people. He hated it.

Carrie Fisher (Princess Leia) and Harrison Ford (Han Solo) on the set of The Empire Strikes Back, *the first sequel to* Star Wars.

gave a crucial new supporting role, Lando Calrissian, to African-American actor Billy Dee Williams, and he was careful to include other minority actors in the cast.

The movie's most important new role—Yoda, the delightful Jedi master—was played by a puppet, not a human. Yoda was created by artist Stuart Freeborn, inspired by a portrait of Albert Einstein and Freeborn's own balding head. The crew that operated the puppet was led by Muppets cofounder Frank Oz, who also "voiced" Yoda.

Leigh Brackett, a veteran Hollywood writer, wrote a screenplay based on Lucas's rough draft. Lucas wanted the writer, whose specialty was witty dialogue, to bring warmth and snap to the dialogue of his basic story. Tragically, Brackett died of cancer two weeks after delivering her draft.

Over the summer of 1978, Lucas worked on polishing the script himself, with little success. Meanwhile, writer Lawrence Kasdan, a relative newcomer to Hollywood, had begun working on a script for a story Lucas was interested in putting together with Steven Spielberg.

Kasdan delivered a first draft of this script to Lucas at his home in Marin County, and over lunch Lucas told the writer about his problems with *Empire*. To Kasdan's astonishment, the producer then asked the writer to polish Brackett's draft. A shocked Kasdan pointed to the script he had just delivered and said, "Don't you want to read this first?" Lucas replied, "Well, if I hate it tonight I'll call you up and take back this offer. But I just get a feeling about people." [74]

Shooting Costs

Shooting on *Empire* began in March 1979 in England and Norway, where a glacier stood in for the film's remote ice planet. As with *Star Wars*, almost immediately the production ran into problems. The Norwegian location shoot—where the average temperature was ten below zero—was hampered by blizzards and other delays. The crew was able to shoot only half of the expected footage.

Meanwhile, at Elstree Studios in England, things were also moving slowly. Unlike Lucas, who rarely departed from his carefully planned shooting schedule, director Kershner often chose to abandon his preproduction planning to follow new ideas at the last minute.

The results were visually striking, and often better than the original ideas, but the production paid a steep price in extra time and money. Lucas, in daily phone contact with Kershner and Kurtz in Europe, kept reminding them that they were spending *his* money; Lucasfilms was bankrolling *Empire*, not an outside studio, and if the movie failed so would Lucas.

Lucas did his best to contain the rapidly escalating costs. Nonetheless, the film's original budget of $15 million had grown to $18.5 before shooting had even begun and rose steeply during the actual filming. Its final cost was $33 million, the biggest single expenditure by an independent filmmaker to date.

"Burn-Out Town"

Meanwhile, back in California, Lucas was overseeing the movie's complex special effects: 605 separate shots, more than twice as many as in *Star Wars*. The work was hampered by Lucas's decision to move ILM away from Los Angeles and closer to his home base in the Bay Area. The move from southern California to San Rafael was slow and chaotic. Crews worked frantically among half-finished facilities to finish shots. A scene in which a swamp creature on Yoda's planet grabs R2-D2 and pulls the feisty little 'droid underwater was shot, out of necessity, in Lucas's swimming pool.

Despite his vow to slow down, Lucas worked frantically at ILM, coming home only briefly to eat and sleep. He was not the only one burning the candle at both ends; for the last five months of the project, ILM was running two shifts a day. Tom Smith, ILM's manager at the time, recalls that virtually everyone on his staff was near the breaking point: "This place was burn-out town." [75]

The publicity and excitement leading up to *Empire*'s opening, in May 1980, were unprecedented. The toll-free number

Just Telling the Story

Steven Spielberg, in his introduction to Charles Champlin's book *George Lucas: The Creative Impulse,* recalls the lesson in simplicity he learned while working with Lucas on *Raiders of the Lost Ark.*

I was determined not to let [anything] get in the way of our fourteen-year-old friendship. So I checked my ego at the door and entered George's world, George's dreams, and I did my utmost to live up to his expectations. . . .

"Don't try to make the greatest movie in the world," he advised during *Raiders* preproduction. "Just get the story told one chapter at a time. Think of this as a B movie."

My last three features: *1941, Close Encounters of the Third Kind,* and *Jaws,* each had taken over 130 days to shoot. George gave me 85 days for *Raiders*—a considerably bigger production than *Close Encounters* or *Jaws*—so with an ear always bent in George's direction, I figured I'd finally best him in one way at least. I shot *Raiders* in 73 days, lean and mean, very few outtakes on the cutting room floor. I just told the story.

that was set up to give fans a preview collapsed under the strain of the volume of calls. Lines for the premiere formed days ahead of time at theaters across the country, including the Egyptian Theater in Los Angeles, where the movie was premiering with a nonstop, twenty-four-hour run.

When the movie was finally shown, the almost universal reaction was ecstatic delight. Lucasfilms recovered its investment within three months, and *Empire* went on to earn over $300 million worldwide. Lucas shared some $5 million of the profits among his cast, crew, and all Lucasfilms employees—even the nighttime janitorial staff.

Raiders

Overlapping with *Empire*'s production was preliminary work on *Raiders of the Lost Ark,* the adventure story Lucas had been working on with Spielberg and Kasdan. It was an affectionate homage to the cliff-hangers Lucas had loved as a kid.

Lucas had told several people about this idea, but few had been enthusiastic. While sitting out the *Star Wars* opening in

George Lucas (left) and Steven Spielberg (right) collaborated in the 1980s on the first in a series of adventure movies beginning with Raiders of the Lost Ark.

Hawaii, however, Lucas had discussed the project with Spielberg while the two worked on a gigantic sand castle. Spielberg loved the idea—especially the roguish hero. He recalls, "When he [Lucas] mentioned that it would be like the old serials and that the guy would wear a soft fedora and carry a bullwhip, I was completely hooked."[76]

With Kasdan, the pair hammered out the details. The story, set before World War II, concerned a race against Nazi agents to find the Ark of the Covenant, the holiest of Jewish relics. The hero, Indiana Jones (named for Marcia Lucas's dog), led a dual life: mild-mannered, academic archaeologist and swashbuckling, slightly shady fortune hunter. This likable rascal may be closer than any other character in a George Lucas film to the filmmaker's own fantasies; Lucas once remarked, "If I could be a dream figure, I'd be Indy."[77]

The two filmmakers complemented each other's strengths. Spielberg's reputation was for going far over budget, and in the wake of his last movie, the expensive bomb *1941*, he stood to benefit from Lucas's financially conservative style. Also, Spielberg loves to direct, while from the outset Lucas only wanted to produce. Spielberg remarks:

> George Lucas is . . . a business genius, as well as a great conceptualizer, and I'm much more of a hard-working drone. I enjoy rolling up my sleeves and getting into it. I think George has fun thinking up ideas and then sitting back and saying, "OK, go off and make it. It's your movie now."[78]

"It's Your Movie"

While shooting *Raiders*, Lucas did not stray from his reputation for finding ways to save money. One story conference centered on how to build the Nazis' elaborate V-wing airplane within budget. Lucas quietly picked up a scale model of the plane and broke off the wing's tips, eliminating two of its engines. This move, in turn, eliminated $250,000 in expense for the full-size plane. For another scene, Lucas talked Spielberg out of using two thousand Arab extras, convincing his friend to settle for six hundred. Lucas joked to Spielberg, "Well, it's your movie. If the audience doesn't like it, they're going to blame you." Spielberg responded, "Okay, but I'm going to tell them that you made me do it."[79]

When *Raiders* was released in 1981, audiences did indeed like it; the worldwide box office take, over $363 million, made it the year's runaway success. The film was nominated for eight Oscars and received five, all in technical categories. Furthermore, it made a superstar out of Harrison Ford, tapped for the role after the original choice, Tom Selleck, was unable to get away from his TV commitments.

Some reviewers found the movie cold and mechanical, but critical reaction was generally ecstatic. Typical was the opinion of Vincent Canby of the *New York Times*, who called it "one of the most deliriously funny, ingenious and stylish American adventure movies ever made."[80]

For Lucas, *Raiders* reawakened his pleasure in filmmaking. First of all, it was a tremendous financial success; since the film had come in on budget and on schedule, he and Spielberg could take advantage of the lucrative deal they had struck with Paramount for a large share of the profits. If the film had run over budget, they would have faced stiff penalties.

More importantly, Lucas realized that he could actually enjoy making movies. Directing took a great deal out of him, but producing—especially when working with someone as attuned to his own sensibilities as Spielberg—could be delightful. "I probably had more fun on that picture than any other," he recalls. "I didn't have to do anything but hang out. I had all the confidence in the world in Steve and I was not at risk financially."[81]

Return of the Jedi

Next in line for Lucasfilms was *Return of the Jedi*, the third installment in the *Star Wars* trilogy.

As he always did when writing a film's story, Lucas listened to suggestions from others, although he did not always take their advice. For instance, Harrison Ford—who was wary of becoming typecast as Han Solo—lobbied unsuccessfully for Lucas to kill his character off. He says, "I had no idea of what to do with my character. [I felt that] since Han Solo had no momma and no

Just Hanging Out

Lucas had a good time making *Raiders of the Lost Ark* with Spielberg; he had almost forgotten, according to this passage in *Skywalking*, that filmmaking could be fun.

> I probably had more fun on that picture than any other. I didn't have to do anything but hang out. I had all the confidence in the world in Steve and I was not at risk financially. I was hoping it would come in on budget, but if it didn't . . . well, for once, I wasn't at risk.

poppa and wasn't going to get the girl anyway, he may as well die to give the whole thing some real emotional resonance."[82]

Lawrence Kasdan again returned to co-write the screenplay with Lucas. However, Lucas's longtime associate Gary Kurtz had left Lucasfilms in the wake of the tensions over *Empire*'s spiraling cost overruns. To produce *Jedi*, Lucas turned again to Howard Kazanjian. The director was Richard Marquand, an Englishman who had impressed Lucas with the craftsmanship of his wartime thriller *Eye of the Needle*.

Secrecy had always been tight on the *Star Wars* sets, but now that the series had become so famous, security reached new heights. In the final weeks of the shoot, in northern California redwood forests, the cast pretended to be working on a horror film called *Blue Harvest*. Curious onlookers saw nothing to suggest a *Star Wars* shoot, only crew members wearing T-shirts that read "Blue Harvest: Horror Beyond Imagination." Lucas joked that the T-shirts really referred to the process of making a movie.

The new film's major plot revelation—that Luke and Princess Leia are brother and sister—was kept secret from even the cast members until the last moment. Carrie Fisher says she was glad the secret was revealed to her before the cameras were rolling: "I'd have laughed on camera if Mark [Hamill] had told me for the first time then."[83]

The Toys Take Over?

Jedi was released in May 1983, six years to the day after *Star Wars*. As expected, it set new box office records: 1.5 million people saw *Jedi* within two days of its release. Its opening total ($6.2

Store shelves abound with Star Wars *merchandise.*

million) was the biggest so far, and its first week's income ($45.3 million) topped that of the then-current record holder, *E.T. Jedi* went on to gross a total of $232 million worldwide.

The premiere was accompanied by a publicity campaign and auxiliary marketing effort even more enormous than those for the previous films. Five *Jedi* books were on the best-seller lists simultaneously, and there were a number of lucrative arcade video games based on the film. The Kenner company's toy catalogue listed forty versions of toys based on the film's cuddly Ewoks alone.

This increased emphasis on marketing disgusted and offended some observers. Critic Peter Rainer complained in the *Los Angeles Herald Examiner*, "This time the toys have taken over the toy store," while *Newsweek*'s David Ansen added, "The innocence that made *Star Wars* the movie phenomenon of the

1970s has long since vanished. It has become its own relentless Empire, grinding out Fun with soulless efficiency."[84]

"A Lot of Fun Things Come Out of It"

Lucas seemed unaffected by the criticism, and he has never apologized for his rapidly expanding marketing empire. Ever since the release of *Star Wars*, in fact, the filmmaker had worked hard to consolidate his merchandising rights.

Over the years, *Star Wars* products have generated an estimated $4 billion, nearly four times as much as the movies themselves. Lucas likes to point out that the profits from merchandising pay for his other activities, which include companies developing state-of-the-art film technology. He remarks, "People tend to look at merchandizing as an evil thing. But ultimately, a lot of fun things come out of it, and at the same time, it pays for the overhead of the company and everybody's salary."[85]

Chapter 7

The Empire Rolls On

The way my father brought me up gave me a lot of the common sense I use to get me through the business world.
—George Lucas

Running the company to me is like mowing the lawn. It has to be done. I semi-enjoy it, once in a while.
—George Lucas

FINANCIALLY SPEAKING, LUCAS does not ever need to make another movie, or even to work in any capacity. According to recent estimates by *Forbes* magazine, Lucasfilms and related companies are together worth about $5 billion; Lucas himself has a personal worth of some $2 billion.

However, Lucas has repeatedly said that he has always wanted to continue making movies. His workaholic tendencies, furthermore, have never let him stay idle for long. Though for years he resisted the urge to resume the exhausting job of directing, he continued to keep active in a variety of ways.

More Indy

When Spielberg and Lucas had first agreed to do *Raiders*, they made an informal "gentleman's agreement": if it was successful, they would make at least two more Indy movies.

In 1984 *Indiana Jones and the Temple of Doom* reunited the writing team of Huyck and Katz with producer Lucas, and Steven Spielberg again directed. *Temple of Doom*, which concerned a sacred Hindu treasure and an evil castle full of enslaved children, cost $30 million, nearly twice the budget of the first Indy movie.

Lucas (left) and Spielberg (right) pose with cast members from the popular Indiana Jones *series.*

It was also much darker and more violent. "George wanted it to be really scary," Huyck recalls. "Steve was leery at first, but then he got into it; and when Steve does something, he does it to the nth degree."[86]

Many parents and critics hated the film's violence, which included such cruel scenes as ripping a man's beating heart out of his body. Protests helped spur the creation of a new rating by the Motion Picture Association of America. Previously, movie ratings had gone from G to PG to R, but now a new rating was added: PG-13, meaning that no one under thirteen could see the film without a parent or guardian.

More successful, at least with the critics, was 1989's *Indiana Jones and the Last Crusade.* Having used Jewish and Hindu relics in their first two stories, Spielberg and Lucas (along with screenwriter Jeffrey Boam) centered *Last Crusade*'s story line on the Holy Grail, sought by Christians since the Middle Ages.

The story also involved Indy's reconciliation with his father, played by the rugged veteran Sean Connery, best known as the actor who created James Bond on screen. The choice was a sly touch, since the character of Indy had been created to both honor and outdo Bond. The two heroes were alike in many re-spects, Connery wryly notes: "Aside from the fact that Indiana Jones is not as well-dressed as James Bond, the main difference between them is [that] Indiana deals with women shyly."[87]

Critics generally applauded *Last Crusade*, noting that it was as thrillingly entertaining as the first Indy movie while avoiding the racist overtones and violence of *Temple of Doom*. Audiences agreed; *Last Crusade* collected $494.7 million worldwide, a bet-ter return than the troubled second movie in the series.

Restoring *American Graffiti* and *Star Wars*

Even while embarking on new projects, Lucas remained ob-sessed with preserving and restoring his early successes. For the twenty-fifth-anniversary rerelease of *American Graffiti*, Lucas was able to restore the minutes that had been cut. He also reshot one scene, digitally improving a shot that had never satisfied him.

Lucasfilms also rereleased the entire *Star Wars* trilogy on video. This "special edition" sold some 30 million copies in a one-time-only event and began the process of introducing *Star Wars* to a new generation.

Lucas then celebrated the twentieth-year anniversary of *Star Wars* with wildly successful theatrical rereleases of all three films.

To celebrate the twentieth anniversary of Star Wars, *Lucas rereleased the entire trilogy, digitally remastered with many new scenes that were cut from the original.*

A new generation saw the films on wide screens for the first time. *Star Wars* reclaimed its title as the highest grossing film of all time, and the three films (counting their rereleases) have now taken in more than $1.5 billion around the world.

The new versions of the films, taking advantage of new technology and a bigger budget for creating effects, have improved visuals. The new touches include enhanced color and sharpness throughout, as well as improved effects such as cleaning up the "Vaseline blob" that once hovered beneath Luke's sand cruiser when it was in motion. There are also about four minutes of new, digitally enhanced footage, including an encounter between Han Solo and the alien loan shark, Jabba the Hutt.

Some film purists complain that these changes alter the impact of the original film for the worse. Mark Altman, editor in chief of *Sci-Fi Universe* magazine, comments, "The insertions are incredibly distracting. . . . Why do this? It sets a very dangerous precedent for the future. If I go see *Casablanca* [released in 1942] in a theater, I want to see a great print. I don't want to see a new computer-generated plane in the airport scene."[88]

Lucas, however, feels fully justified in tinkering with his films. He remarks, "My feeling is, an artist is allowed to work on his projects until such time as he dies."[89]

Overseeing the Action Figures

Lucas was busy during this period in many other ways. Overseeing the world of licensing *Star Wars* toys alone would be enough for many businessmen, since this enterprise changed the face of movie marketing forever and continues to be a juggernaut.

Before *Star Wars*, merchandise was used only to promote movies and had no value apart from advertising the films. But thanks to the unprecedented demand for *Star Wars* products, movie merchandising became an enormous business unto itself. *Star Wars* merchandising paved the way for more recent phenomena such as the Warner Brothers Studio Store, Power Rangers, and the seventeen thousand separate *101 Dalmatians* products that Disney has licensed.

Nonetheless, *Star Wars* remains the biggest single movie merchandising project in history. In addition to the money the

Not Warm and Fuzzy

Lucas has always been extremely shy, and he rarely gives out praise. His employees have become used to his brusque manner, but it can still be a source of aggravation. In this passage from Garry Jenkins's *Empire Building*, Jim Nelson, a founding executive of Industrial Light & Magic, puts it this way:

> He'd just walk by you in the hall and never say a word. He lives in his own world, he's not a warm, friendly guy. George is very critical, so you know, when he didn't like something, you'd know in a minute. He'd tell you "I hate it.". . . I like George. But George is very difficult to work with; you must agree with George and if you don't agree with George then George doesn't like you.

trilogy has earned in ticket sales to date, more than $3 billion has been earned in licensing fees. In 1996, for example, *Star Wars* action figures were the best-selling toy for boys and the second overall best-seller after Barbie.

Not all these toys are bought to be played with. The value of certain *Star Wars* toys as collectors' items grows daily. A large percentage of *Star Wars* action figures are bought by merchandise dealers, who hoard them in hopes that their price will rise. As a result, it has often been so difficult to find *Star Wars* toys that some stores have set limits on the number of action figures one person can buy.

Other Projects

The *Star Wars* and Indiana Jones franchises were by no means Lucas's only projects throughout the 1980s and 1990s. He also kept busy as a producer of a variety of other films.

He produced a lavish sci-fi comedy, *Howard the Duck*, based on a popular underground comic strip and written by Huyck and Katz. It did not find favor at the box office, however, and proved to be an expensive bomb. Lucas also wrote and produced a nostalgic mystery-comedy set in a 1930s radio station, *The Radioland Murders*. The fast-moving *Radioland* also bombed, and Lucas wondered aloud if critics had judged it too harshly because of his fame. He defended *Radioland*'s "small" stature, saying, "Movies like *Radioland Murders* don't fall into the art market, but they don't fall into the blockbuster, superstar market, either." [90]

More successful, in the eyes of many, were some of Lucas's other producing projects. These included full-length animations: *Twice upon a Time*, created by longtime friend John Korty, and the animated feature *Land Before Time*, and fantasies. In the latter category were *Labyrinth*, the directorial debut of Muppets co-founder Jim Henson, and the charming *Willow*, directed by Ron Howard from a story by Lucas.

Despite his childhood love of television, Lucas had become slightly disdainful of the medium over the years. Nonetheless, he did make occasional forays into TV production. The most successful of these were *The Young Indiana Jones Chronicles* and a series of TV movies, *The Ewok Adventures*, starring the adorable furry creatures that had been featured in *Jedi*.

Lucas has long had an interest in helping other filmmakers get their projects made, often lending his name to an otherwise dubious project. For example, he signed on as executive producer

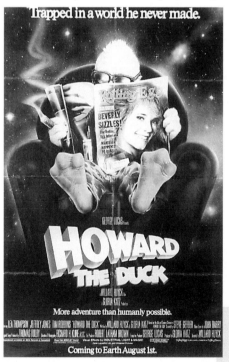

Lucas's lavish science fiction comedy Howard the Duck *was a box office failure.*

of *Latino*, a political drama directed by his longtime friend, cinematographer Haskell Wexler. Lucas overcame the distance that had developed between himself and another old friend, Francis Coppola, and agreed to produce Coppola's excellent drama *Tucker: The Man and His Dream*. (Ironically, Lucas had eclipsed his former mentor in terms of Hollywood clout; now it was Lucas's name that guaranteed a project would see the light of day.)

Lucas and Coppola coproduced *Mishima*, a film by Paul Schrader about controversial Japanese novelist Yukio Mishima. Lucas and Coppola also teamed up with singer/dancer Michael Jackson, then at the height of his popularity, to create a lavish but brief extravaganza, *Captain EO*, for Disneyland.

Sometimes, Lucas has helped filmmakers not by acting as executive producer but by directly raising money. For example, when the master Japanese director Akira Kurosawa could not complete his epic films *Kagemusha* and *Dreams*, Lucas teamed with Spielberg and Coppola to raise funding. Lucas says, "There is a whole group of us who have a strong wish to help others, either young directors who haven't yet had a shot at it, or older directors who've been passed by but who still have creative ideas."[91]

George Lucas and Francis Ford Coppola at the ribbon-cutting ceremony for their film Captain EO.

"They're All Interesting"

In Charles Champlin's book *George Lucas: The Creative Impulse*, the filmmaker reflects on the many often overlooked projects he has been involved with since *Star Wars*.

> On the one hand I'm doing these huge productions and at the same time I'm helping on these little productions, for my friends. They're all interesting movies, movies that I cared about and wanted to see made one way or another. Some of them were small failures, some of them were huge failures and some were extremely nice movies. But in most of the interviews with me, and even within the company [Lucasfilms], they're passed right over, as though they never existed. But those movies may be closer to what I am than *Star Wars*.

More High Tech

A major aspect of Lucas's "retirement" has been his use of his wealth to foster filmmaking, especially in exploring the frontiers of high-technology cinema. He has made, for instance, a series of multi-million-dollar gifts toward a new film facility at USC, his alma mater. In addition, he has poured still more millions into creating a rapidly expanding, interrelated family of high-tech companies.

These companies have overall been profitable ventures for Lucas; however, as he likes to point out, if he were interested in profit only, there would be many better ways for him to make money. Making a long-term impact on the film industry has been of greater importance to him. "It's a creative community," Lucas says of his interrelated companies, which are all centered near his home in northern California. "And me having access to this creative community is what the real dividend of all this is."[92]

One aspect of this experimentation has been the development of interactive computer video games for the home. LucasArts Entertainment has become one of the world's largest makers of video games for computers, including such best sellers as Rebel Assault, X-Wing, and Dark Forces.

Most of Lucas's experiments, however, have been in more traditional realms of cinema. One example of this is Skywalker Sound, which began as a sound effects company and later branched out to develop highly sophisticated sound systems for theaters and homes under the name THX, in honor of Lucas's first movie.

The best-known of Lucas's high-tech companies is still Industrial Light & Magic. Since its genesis working on Lucas-related films, ILM has expanded into an effects for-hire company to other studios and filmmakers.

Over the years, ILM has remained the preeminent company in its field, creating effects for many of Hollywood's most spectacular films, including *Jurassic Park* and *Twister.* Along the way, the company has spawned dozens of other companies, as employees leave to form their own firms. Steven Spielberg acknowledges the significance of ILM and Lucas's other high-tech companies when he says, "George Lucas has the best toys of anybody I have ever known, which is why it's so much fun playing over at George's house."[93]

Skywalker Ranch

Ever since his film school days, Lucas had dreamed of establishing a self-contained moviemaking center away from the hustle of Hollywood. Displaying an attitude acquired from his father, Lucas says of the established Hollywood community: "Down there, for every honest filmmaker trying to get his film off the ground, there are a hundred sleazy used-car dealers trying to con you out of your money."[94]

He and others had unsuccessfully tried to establish such an idyllic spot with American Zoetrope. When *Star Wars* provided the financial resources to go it alone, Lucas was finally able to begin putting together his dream. It would put all his interrelated high-tech companies together into one state-of-the-art facility, to be called Skywalker Ranch.

Lucas began buying land for Skywalker soon after the release of *Star Wars* in 1977. Today, this nerve center of his business empire comprises some three thousand acres of rolling countryside in the Lucas Valley of Marin County. (The name is coincidental.)

Lucas has spent at least $75 million developing the ranch and is still overseeing constant expansions and improvements. The filmmaker says he thinks of it as a large-scale creative project: "It's my biggest movie. I've always been a frustrated architect."[95]

Rural Feel

Lucas made up an extensive "history" for each building, which gave his architects a guide to the feel he wanted to create. He also carefully mapped the area so that only one or two other buildings can be seen from any given spot.

Lucasfilms's offices and studios are housed in this complex of antique-looking houses, built in a mixture of Victorian, craftsman, and other architectural styles. An enormous mansion, the Big House, serves as the centerpiece. A building that looks like a winery is actually the site of advanced postproduction facilities. Tucked around in similar buildings are a day-care center, a gym, and other amenities for the staff.

Despite the development, Lucas has gone to great lengths to maintain Skywalker Ranch's rural feel. Mountain lions and bobcats live in the hills around the ranch, and cattle roam its meadows. Several thousand trees were especially chosen and planted to create a habitat for foxes, pheasants, and other wildlife. Few cars are noticeable on the ranch's roads or near its buildings; a vast underground parking garage hides them.

The Skywalker Ranch is a three-thousand-acre, state-of-the-art filmmaking facility nestled in the beautiful Lucas Valley of Marin County, California.

Lucas and his colleagues have high expectations of the people they hire to work at Skywalker Ranch, but dressing for success is not a requirement. The dress code is as casual as that of the boss's trademark flannel shirt, jeans, and sneakers.

People good enough to work at Skywalker Ranch can usually find higher-paying jobs elsewhere in the film industry, since Lucas generally pays less than his competitors, and offers little in the way of stock or other incentives. But life at the ranch offers them a more easy-going pace than they would find in Los Angeles, as well as a utopian setting and the prestige of collaborating with the famed Lucas. Journalist David Kaplan summarizes Lucas's architectural creation by noting that the filmmaker "may only be the 56th-richest person in America, according to the *Forbes* list, but he's got the best workplace around."[96]

Separation and Divorce

A major change in the filmmaker's private life came shortly after the release of *Jedi* in 1983, when he and his wife announced that they were separating. The Lucases had seemed like a stable couple, but the marriage had apparently been strained for several years. In part, the problem seems to have stemmed from Lucas's workaholic tendencies.

Although he had promised to cut back after *Star Wars* and especially after the Lucases adopted a baby, Amanda, the filmmaker was unable to keep away from his work. Marcia Lucas comments, "For me, the bottom line was just that he was all work and no play. I felt that we paid our dues [and now] I wanted joy in my life. And George . . . wanted to stay on that workaholic track. The empire builder, the dynamo. And I couldn't see myself living that way for the rest of my life."[97]

There was also a growing incompatibility in tastes. Marcia loved to go out, to have friends over for dinner, to meet new people. Lucas, however, disliked going out; one associate has commented that the filmmaker's idea of a good time was watching TV while eating a tunafish sandwich. He did not like to spend much time with anyone other than the small group of friends and collaborators he had known for years.

When the Lucases decided to divorce, the settlement reportedly cost Lucas $50 million, although by some accounts the filmmaker was less concerned about money than other matters. Lucas insisted that he have custody of the couple's young daughter. He also insisted that he keep his beloved Skywalker Ranch.

Single Father

In the years since his divorce, Lucas adopted two more children: a daughter, Katie, and a son, Jett. During that time, the filmmaker apparently had only one serious romantic relationship.

Lucas's intensely private life, as single father and moviemaker-businessman, seems to suit him well. The filmmaker says that his new role has led to a reorganization of priorities. He remarks, "It used to be that movies were everything in my life. I ate, slept, lived movies 24 hours a day, seven days a week. And then my children came along and movies became the No. 2 priority."[98]

In recent years, Lucas has begun spending only a day or two a week at Skywalker Ranch. The rest of the time is devoted to

Lucas and two of his three adopted children, Amanda (left) and Katie (center).

Listening to the Flies

In this passage from his 1997 interview in *Playboy*, Lucas comments on his dislike for high technology in daily life.

For being sort of a state-of-the-art guy, my personal life is very unstate-of-the-art. It's Victorian, actually. I like to sit on a porch and listen to the flies buzz if I have five minutes, because most of my life is interacting with people all the time. I interact with a couple hundred people every day, and it's very intense. I have three kids, so I interact with them during whatever's left of the day. The few brief seconds I have before I fall asleep are usually more meditative in nature.

his private life. Although daily life has obviously changed as a result of his financial success, Lucas's tastes remain simple, and he lives modestly compared to some others with great wealth. Lucas explains, "The focus of my life, the thing I care about, was and is making movies. And what sustains you through a time of poverty, which was the first ten years, also sustains you in a time of wealth. . . . There's never been a period when money was a major focus for me."[99]

In 1994 Lucas emerged from his reclusive life to grant a rare series of interviews. He was motivated by the announcement his millions of fans had long been waiting for: the production of a new cycle of *Star Wars* films.

Epilogue

Into the Future

It took me a long time to adjust to Star Wars. *I finally did, and I'm going back to it.* Star Wars *is my destiny.*

—George Lucas

*S*TAR *W*ARS FANS knew that the three existing movies were only part of a longer saga. Rumors that more films were in production had surfaced ever since the release of *Jedi.*

Finally, in May 1994—over a decade since *Jedi's* release—Lucas revealed that he was writing three new segments, "prequels" that fill in the story preceding the existing films. Even more electrifying was the news that Lucas would direct at least the first of these himself, the first time he had directed a movie since *Star Wars* in 1977.

New Fever

Lucas's announcement said that this first prequel would appear in 1999, with the others tentatively scheduled for 2001 and 2003. If he holds to this schedule, the director will be 75 years old when the sixth completed film is released, and he is doubtful that he will direct the others.

Immediately following Lucas's announcement of the planned prequels, gossip began on the Internet and elsewhere, speculating on issues such as casting the new film. One false rumor asserted that Charlton Heston would play a Jedi knight. In the end, Lucas chose an international cast, including the Irish actor Liam Neeson, Scotsman Ewan McGregor, and Americans Natalie Portman, Jake Lloyd, and Samuel L. Jackson.

By the time *Star Wars: Episode I: The Phantom Menace* premiered in May 1999, *Star Wars* fever was as high—or higher—than ever. When a two-minute trailer for the film was shown in the fall of 1998 at the beginning of feature films across the country, thousands of loyal fans paid admission to see it—and then walked out. They were not interested in the feature, only in Lucas's trailer. When the same trailer was presented on Apple Computer's Web site, more than a million fans downloaded it the first day. And nearly a thousand sites on the World Wide Web were devoted to *Star Wars*, including one set up by fans waiting in line for tickets to the film's Los Angeles premiere.

As might be expected, *Phantom Menace* was accompanied by dozens of products based on new characters and creatures, including a multi-billion-dollar promotion tied to fast-food restaurant chains and soda companies. According to some sources that track advertising, it was the biggest merchandising campaign in history. According to Jim Silver, editor of the trade publication *Toy Book*, "The consensus is that the new toys alone will make more than a billion dollars in [only one year] 1999."[100]

What He Learned

In keeping with his reputation for making movies with a minimum of wasted effort, Lucas reportedly plans to spend no more on each movie than $100 million, a modest figure considering that some productions with similarly sky-high budgets have disappeared without a trace. As before, Lucas is retaining maximum control over the new films, funding their production himself and retaining all rights.

In large part, advances in technology inspired Lucas to film more *Star Wars* episodes. Improved digital computer graphics and other techniques will let him create, with relative ease and economy, exactly what he envisions. He remarks of ILM's breakthroughs, "Suddenly all the constraints are lifted. It's like you've been plowing fields in one-hundred-degree sun, with a seventy-pound backpack and lead balls chained to your ankles, and someone comes along and puts you in an air-conditioned tractor."[101]

Loyal fans camped for days and even weeks to be the first to see the new installment of the Star Wars *saga,* The Phantom Menace.

Although special effects will remain highlights of the films, Lucas intends to focus equally on character and plot development. These are areas in which he feels he has been deficient. As a filmmaker, Lucas has often said, he has always concentrated on telling a story with maximum speed, efficiency, and visual style. From watching others direct his films, however, he learned that fast pacing and flashy visuals are not the only important parts of filmmaking. He promises both flair and depth in his new works: "Just as *Star Wars* gave you something you knew you'd never seen before, that's what I'm hoping for in the new movies." [102]

More of the *Star Wars* saga, a long-rumored fourth Indiana Jones film, or movies now playing only in his mind's eye—no matter which of these reaches the screen in the next one thousand years, it seems clear that George Lucas's vision will reach startling new heights.

Notes

Introduction: Building Dreams and Empires

1. Quoted in Bernard Weinraub, "Luke Skywalker Goes Home," *Playboy*, July 1997.
2. David Thomson, "Who Killed the Movies?" *Esquire*, December 1996.
3. Quoted in David A. Kaplan, "The Force Is Still with Us," *Newsweek*, January 20, 1997.
4. Quoted in Weinraub, "Luke Skywalker Goes Home."

Chapter 1: Modesto: A Long Time Ago in a Galaxy Far, Far Away . . .

5. Quoted in Dale Pollock, *Skywalking: The Life and Films of George Lucas*. New York: Harmony, 1983, p. 15.
6. Quoted in Charles Champlin, *George Lucas: The Creative Impulse*. New York: Harry Abrams, 1992, p. 16.
7. Quoted in Garry Jenkins, *Empire Building*, Secaucus, NJ: Citadel Press, 1997, p. 2.
8. Quoted in Jenkins, *Empire Building*, p. 4.
9. Quoted in Jenkins, *Empire Building*, p. 8.
10. Quoted in Weinraub, "Luke Skywalker Goes Home."
11. Quoted in Pollock, *Skywalking*, p. 37.
12. Quoted in Weinraub, "Luke Skywalker Goes Home."
13. Quoted in Pollock, *Skywalking*, p. 24.
14. Quoted in Weinraub, "Luke Skywalker Goes Home."
15. Quoted in Weinraub, "Luke Skywalker Goes Home."
16. Quoted in Pollock, *Skywalking*, p. xvi.

Chapter 2: Film School

17. Quoted in Peter Biskind, *Easy Riders, Raging Bulls: How the Sex-Drugs-and-Rock 'n' Roll Generation Saved Hollywood*. New York: Simon & Schuster, 1998, p. 317.

18. Quoted in Pollock, *Skywalking*, p. 39.
19. Quoted in Pollock, *Skywalking*, p. 42.
20. Quoted in Michael Pye and Lynda Myles, *The Movie Brats: How the Film Generation Took Over Hollywood.* New York: Holt, Rinehart & Winston, 1979, p. 114.
21. Jenkins, *Empire Building*, p. 11.
22. Quoted in Pollock, *Skywalking*, p. 45.
23. Quoted in Jenkins, *Empire Building*, p. 11.
24. Quoted in Pollock, *Skywalking*, p. 55.
25. Quoted in Pollock, *Skywalking*, p. 57.
26. Quoted in Jenkins, *Empire Building*, p. 12.
27. Quoted in Pye and Myles, *The Movie Brats*, p. 9.
28. Quoted in Joseph McBride, *Steven Spielberg: A Biography.* New York: Simon & Schuster, 1997, p. 137.

Chapter 3: American Zoetrope and *THX 1138*

29. Quoted in Pollock, *Skywalking*, p. 65.
30. Quoted in Champlin, *George Lucas*, p. 18.
31. Quoted in Pollock, *Skywalking*, pp. 68–69.
32. Quoted in Champlin, *George Lucas*, p. 9.
33. Quoted in Jenkins, *Empire Building*, p. 16.
34. Quoted in Pye and Myles, *The Movie Brats*, p. 81.
35. Quoted in Pye and Myles, *The Movie Brats*, p. 116.
36. Quoted in Champlin, *George Lucas*, p. 19.
37. Quoted in Jenkins, *Empire Building*, p. 20.
38. Quoted in Champlin, *George Lucas*, p. 24.
39. Quoted in Pye and Myles, *The Movie Brats*, p. 119.
40. Quoted in Chris Nashawaty, "'American Graffiti': Has It Really Been a Quarter Century Since This Classic Youth Movie Went to the Oscars?" *Entertainment Weekly*, March 1, 1999.

Chapter 4: American Graffiti

41. Quoted in Pye and Myles, *The Movie Brats*, p. 127.
42. Quoted in Champlin, *George Lucas*, p. 30.
43. Quoted in Champlin, *George Lucas*, p. 30.
44. Quoted in Pollock, *Skywalking*, p. 105.
45. Quoted in Champlin, *George Lucas*, p. 26.
46. Quoted in Nashawaty, "'American Graffiti.'"
47. Quoted in Pollock, *Skywalking*, p. 115.

48. Quoted in Nashawaty, "'American Graffiti.'"
49. Quoted in Jenkins, *Empire Building*, p. 32.
50. Quoted in Nashawaty, "'American Graffiti.'"
51. Quoted in Pollock, *Skywalking*, p. 121.
52. Quoted in Nashawaty, "'American Graffiti.'"
53. Peter Bart, "'George and Francis Show' Returns; Twenty-Five Years After 'American Graffiti,' Lucas and Coppola Seem Re-energized as They Embark on Separate Strategies," *Variety*, July 27, 1998.
54. Quoted in Champlin, *George Lucas*, p. 35.
55. Quoted in Nashawaty, "'American Graffiti.'"

Chapter 5: *Star Wars*

56. Quoted in Weinraub, "Luke Skywalker Goes Home."
57. Quoted in Biskind, *Easy Riders, Raging Bulls*, p. 319.
58. Quoted in Nashawaty, "'American Graffiti.'"
59. Quoted in Champlin, *George Lucas*, p. 42.
60. Quoted in *Time*, "The Force Is Back: With 'Star Wars,' George Lucas Played to Our Fantasies; Now, As the New Version Is Released, He Reveals His," February 10, 1997.
61. Quoted in Jenkins, *Empire Building*, p. 52.
62. Quoted in Champlin, *George Lucas*, p. 42.
63. Quoted in Biskind, *Easy Riders, Raging Bulls*, p. 326.
64. Quoted in Jenkins, *Empire Building*, p. 97.
65. Quoted in Pollock, *Skywalking*, p. 162.
66. Quoted in Champlin, *George Lucas*, p. 49.
67. Quoted in Pye and Myles, *The Movie Brats*, p. 135.
68. Quoted in Pollock, *Skywalking*, p. 176.
69. Quoted in Biskind, *Easy Riders, Raging Bulls*, p. 335.
70. Quoted in Pollock, *Skywalking*, p. 182.
71. Quoted in Biskind, *Easy Riders, Raging Bulls*, p. 336.
72. Quoted in Jenkins, *Empire Building*, p. 124.

Chapter 6: Life After *Star Wars*

73. Quoted in Champlin, *George Lucas*, p. 59.
74. Quoted in Champlin, *George Lucas*, p. 65.
75. Quoted in Pollock, *Skywalking*, p. 216.
76. Quoted in Champlin, *George Lucas*, p. 79.
77. Quoted in McBride, *Steven Spielberg*, p. 312.
78. Quoted in Frank Sanello, *Spielberg: The Man, the Movies, the Mythology*. Dallas, TX: Taylor Publishing, 1996, p. 101.

79. Quoted in McBride, *Steven Spielberg*, p. 319.
80. Quoted in Douglas Brode, *The Films of Steven Spielberg*. New York: Citadel Press, 1995, p. 90.
81. Quoted in Pollock, *Skywalking*, p. 230.
82. Quoted in Champlin, *George Lucas*, p. 94.
83. Quoted in Jenkins, *Empire Building*, p. 244.
84. Quoted in Jenkins, *Empire Building*, p. 251.
85. Quoted in Jenkins, *Empire Building*, p. 251.

Chapter 7: The Empire Rolls On

86. Quoted in Champlin, *George Lucas*, p. 100.
87. Quoted in McBride, *Steven Spielberg*, p. 402.
88. Quoted in Steve Daly, "The Remaking of 'Star Wars,'" *Entertainment Weekly*, January 10, 1997.
89. Quoted in *Entertainment Weekly*, "Lucas Skywasher (George Lucas Improves a Shot Used in 'American Graffiti' with a Computer)," October 2, 1998.
90. Quoted in Glenn Lovell, "George Lucas Has a New Mission: Talking Sense into Hollywood Establishment," Knight-Ridder/Tribune News Service, October 21, 1994.
91. Quoted in Champlin, *George Lucas*, p. 76.
92. Quoted in Randall Lane and James Samuelson, "The Magician," *Forbes*, March 11, 1996.
93. Quoted in Champlin, *George Lucas*, p. vi.
94. Quoted in Weinraub, "Luke Skywalker Goes Home."
95. Quoted in Weinraub, "Luke Skywalker Goes Home."
96. David A. Kaplan, "The Force Is Still with Us," *Newsweek*, January 20, 1997.
97. Quoted in Biskind, *Easy Riders, Raging Bulls*, p. 422.
98. Quoted in Lovell, "George Lucas Has a New Mission."
99. Quoted in Champlin, *George Lucas*, p. 57.

Epilogue: Into the Future

100. Quoted in *Entertainment Weekly*, "Wars Games: Toys, Fast Food, CDs, Books . . . The 'Phantom Menace' Product Blitz Promises to Be an Unstoppable Force," March 5, 1999.
101. Quoted in Jenkins, *Empire Building*, p. 267.
102. Quoted in Kaplan, "The Force Is Still with Us."

Important Dates in the Life of George Lucas

1944
George Walton Lucas Jr. is born in Modesto, California, on May 14.

1962
Graduates from high school after being seriously injured in a car crash.

1964
Receives an AA degree from Modesto Junior College; enters film school at the University of Southern California.

1966
Graduates from USC film school; is rejected for medical reasons from military draft; meets Marcia Griffin while both are working as film editors.

1967
Reenters USC as graduate student; makes influential short film, *THX 1138*.

1967–1969
Works closely with Francis Ford Coppola on several projects, including *The Rain People*.

1969
Weds Marcia Griffin; relocates to Bay Area; begins American Zoetrope collective with Coppola.

1971
Releases feature-length version of *THX*.

1973
Releases *American Graffiti.*

1977
Releases *Star Wars;* begins buying land for what will become Skywalker Ranch.

1979
Releases *More American Graffiti.*

1980
Releases *The Empire Strikes Back.*

1981
Releases *Raiders of the Lost Ark.*

1983
Releases *Return of the Jedi;* divorces Marcia Lucas.

1983–1999
Acts as executive producer for several television series and films, including *The Radioland Murders* and *Willow.*

1984
Releases *Indiana Jones and the Temple of Doom.*

1989
Releases *Indiana Jones and the Last Crusade.*

1994
Announces production of three new *Star Wars* movies.

1997
Releases digitally restored twentieth-anniversary edition of *Star Wars.*

1999
Releases *The Phantom Menace*, first of three new *Star Wars* prequels.

For Further Reading

Mary S. Henderson, *Star Wars: The Magic of Myth.* New York: Bantam, 1997. This book is a companion to the *Star Wars* exhibition at the National Air and Space Museum in Washington, D.C.

D. L. Mabery, *George Lucas.* Minneapolis: Lerner Publications, 1987. A biography for young readers.

David West Reynolds, *Star Wars: The Visual Dictionary.* New York: DK Publishing, 1998. A heavily illustrated and detailed look at the *Star Wars* universe.

Larry Weinberg, *Star Wars: The Making of the Movie.* New York: Random House, 1980. This book for young adults focuses on the film's revolutionary special effects.

Works Consulted

Books

Peter Biskind, *Easy Riders, Raging Bulls: How the Sex-Drugs-and-Rock 'n' Roll Generation Saved Hollywood.* New York: Simon & Schuster, 1998. A tell-all book about the so-called movie brats—George Lucas's generation of filmmakers—who helped overturn the studio system in Hollywood.

Douglas Brode, *The Films of Steven Spielberg.* New York: Citadel Press, 1995. This look at Steven Spielberg's movies (several of which were collaborations with Lucas) is a useful resource.

Charles Champlin, *George Lucas: The Creative Impulse.* New York: Harry Abrams, 1992. A large-format retrospective of Lucas's first twenty years as a filmmaker, with a brief introduction by Steven Spielberg.

Roger Ebert and Gene Siskel, *The Future of the Movies.* Kansas City: Andrews & McMeel, 1991. Lengthy interviews by the distinguished critics with three influential directors: Steven Spielberg, Martin Scorsese, and George Lucas.

Garry Jenkins, *Empire Building.* Secaucus, NJ: Citadel Press, 1997. A rather dry account of the making of the *Star Wars* empire and its effect on Hollywood.

Joseph McBride, *Steven Spielberg: A Biography.* New York: Simon & Schuster, 1997. The best single biography of Spielberg, with many references to Lucas.

Dale Pollock, *Skywalking: The Life and Films of George Lucas.* New York: Harmony, 1983. To date, the only full biography of Lucas.

103

Michael Pye and Lynda Myles, *The Movie Brats: How the Film Generation Took Over Hollywood.* New York: Holt, Rinehart & Winston, 1979. Two British journalists look at an influential generation of film directors.

Frank Sanello, *Spielberg: The Man, the Movies, the Mythology.* Dallas, TX: Taylor Publishing, 1996. A book about Steven Spielberg written by a writer who specializes in show business, with frequent references to Lucas.

Periodicals

Laura A. Ackley, "ILM Harnesses the Force for 'Star Wars' Prequel," *Variety,* July 20, 1998.

Peter Bart, "'George and Francis Show' Returns; Twenty-Five Years After 'American Graffiti,' Lucas and Coppola Seem Re-energized as They Embark on Separate Strategies," *Variety,* July 27, 1998.

Judy Brennan, "Fox Feels the Force," *Entertainment Weekly*, April 17, 1998.

Steve Daly, "May the 4th Be with You," *Entertainment Weekly,* June 13, 1997.

————, "The Remaking of 'Star Wars,'" *Entertainment Weekly,* January 10, 1997.

Entertainment Weekly, "Lucas Skywasher (George Lucas Improves a Shot Used in 'American Graffiti' with a Computer)," October 2, 1998.

————, "Star Wars Watch," September 18, 1998.

————, "Wars Games: Toys, Fast Food, CDs, Books . . . The 'Phantom Menace' Product Blitz Promises to Be an Unstoppable Force," March 5, 1999.

David Freedman, "Starman," *Inc.,* June 15, 1995.

Jeff Jensen, "'Star Wars' '99 to Build Slowly; Starts with Kids," *Advertising Age*, August 31, 1998.

Brian Jones, "Lost in Space," *People Weekly*, February 26, 1996.

David A. Kaplan, "The Force Is Still with Us," *Newsweek,* January 20, 1997.

Randall Lane and James Samuelson, "The Magician," *Forbes*, March 11, 1996.

Glenn Lovell, "George Lucas Has a New Mission: Talking Sense into Hollywood Establishment," Knight-Ridder/Tribune News Service, October 21, 1994.

Kim Masters, "The Lucas Wars: Everyone in Hollywood Is Dying to Sign Up His Next Space Trilogy," *Time*, September 30, 1996.

Anna Mulrine, "Spiffier Ships and a Slug that Speaks: Souped-Up 'Star Wars,'" *U.S. News & World Report*, February 3, 1997.

Chris Nashawaty, "'American Graffiti': Has It Really Been a Quarter Century Since This Classic Youth Movie Went to the Oscars?" *Entertainment Weekly*, March 1, 1999.

———, "Back to the Future: Twenty Years Later, the Empire Strikes Again," *Entertainment Weekly*, August 2, 1996.

People Weekly, "Not So Far, Far Away (Previews for 'Star Wars: Episode 1—The Phantom Menace')," November 30, 1998.

Orville Schell, "A Galaxy of Myth, Money and Kids," *New York Times*, March 21, 1999.

———, "'I'm a Cynic Who Has Hope for the Human Race,'" *New York Times*, March 21, 1999.

Lisa Schwarzbaum, "'Radioland Murders,'" *Entertainment Weekly*, November 4, 1994.

John Seabrook, "Why Is the Force Still with Us?" *The New Yorker*, January 6, 1997.

David Thomson, "Who Killed the Movies?" *Esquire*, December 1996.

Time, "The Force Is Back: With 'Star Wars,' George Lucas Played to Our Fantasies; Now, As the New Version Is Released, He Reveals His," February 10, 1997.

Bernard Weinraub, "Luke Skywalker Goes Home," *Playboy*, July 1997.

Index

Picture Credits

About the Author

Adam Woog has written many books for adults and young adults, including, for Lucent Books, a biography of George Lucas's friend and sometime collaborator Steven Spielberg. Woog lives in his hometown of Seattle, Washington, with his wife and young daughter.